The Gig Bag Book of
ARPEGGIOS
for all Guitarists

Contains 240 arpeggios, in all twelve keys, presented in standard notation and tablature. Plus a handy fretboard diagram that illustrates each arpeggio pattern all over the neck.

Compiled by
Mark Bridges and Joe Dineen

T0033810

Amsco Publications
New York/London/Sydney

Gibson Switchmaster on cover owned by Scot Arch
Cover photograph by William Draffen

Project editor: Ed Lozano
Compiled and edited by Joe Dineen
Music engraving by Mark Bridges

Order No. AM 946902
US International Standard Book Number: 0.8256.1659.X
UK International Standard Book Number: 0.7119.6880.2

Exclusive Distributors:
Music Sales Corporation
257 Park Avenue South, New York, NY 10010 USA
Music Sales Limited
8/9 Frith Street, London W1V 5TZ England
Music Sales Pty. Limited
120 Rothschild Street, Rosebery, Sydney, NSW 2018, Australia

Printed in the United States of America by
Vicks Lithograph and Printing Corporation

Contents

Introduction

This book is a reference guide for guitarists. It is not intended as a method book, but rather as a reference book of arpeggios that are easily accessible to the beginner or advanced guitarist. Regardless of your musical interest, this book contains the majority of arpeggiated chords you will encounter in most styles of music (rock, jazz, country, or blues). Strong knowledge of arpeggios will help build familiarity with the fretboard and help develop flexibility in solo, accompaniment or ensemble playing.

The twenty arpeggiated chord types covered in this book are:

- major
- 6
- maj7
- maj9
- maj9(♯11)
- minor
- m6
- m7
- m9
- m11
- m(maj7)
- 7
- 9
- 7♭9
- 7♯9
- 9♯11
- 7♭5
- 7+
- m7♭5
- °7

The Gig Bag Book of Arpeggios has been designed with the player in mind. You don't have to break the spine of the book to get it to stay open and it doesn't take up all the space on your music stand. It is easy-to-carry and easy-to-use. We hope that this book will serve as a valuable reference source during your years as a developing guitarist.

How to Use this Book

It is strongly recommended that you develop a practice regimen in which you devote some time to arpeggio study. If you practice one hour each session, then devote fifteen or twenty minutes to arpeggio study. Another approach would be to practice your warm-up exercises with a different arpeggio type each day.

Here are some helpful tips:

- Use the handy thumb index to find the key you're looking for.
- At the top of each page you will find the name of the arpeggiated chord. To the right you will find the chord spelled out on the treble staff.
- Notice there are four suggested arpeggio types along with their fingerings. (The arpeggio types and fingerings are only suggested guidelines; you are encouraged to develop your own arpeggio types and fingerings).
- Each variation begins on the root, third, fifth and sixth or seventh degree of the chord.
- The arpeggio types are written in both standard notation and *tablature*. You will find a fretboard diagram at the bottom of the page displaying the arpeggio pattern (the root of the arpeggio appears as a circle, while the other arpeggio tones appear as black dots).
- In addition, the four arpeggio types are bracketed at the top of the fretboard diagram to help you visualize the arpeggio pattern all over the neck.

As for the fingerings in this book, it is my philosophy that the stretches (which may seem difficult) will enable the player to more easily expand the range of the arpeggio to higher and lower registers, thus not limiting the player to "box type" possitioning. Also, the arpeggios are designed to be played in the middle four strings where possible in order to show the inner movement of the voices. You can expand these arpeggios to the outer E-strings by adding notes in the chord stack on the top of the page. You can also workout your own particular fingerings if you find these uncomfortable. Remember these fingerings are optional and I encourage you, the player, to be as creative as possible in creating your own fingering styles.

The chords presented in this book can also be found in *The Gig Bag Book of GuitarTab Chords* where over 2100+ chord variations are presented. As with all books in *The Gig Bag series*, this book can be used as a valuable stand alone reference or enhanced by other titles in the series.

Whether you are looking to develop *chops* (technique) or broaden your arpeggio and chord vocabulary, *The Gig Bag Book of Arpeggios* is for you.

C

Type 1

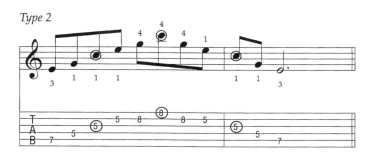

Type 2

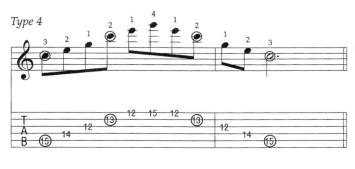

Type 3

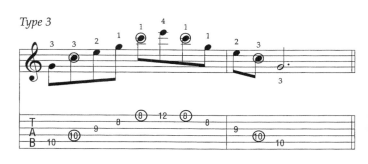

Type 4

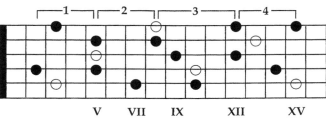

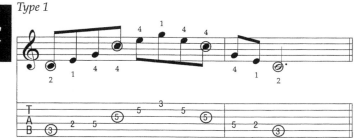

C6

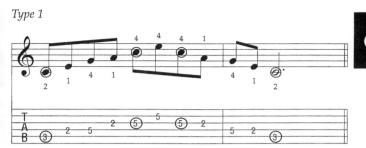

Type 1

Type 2

Type 3

Type 4

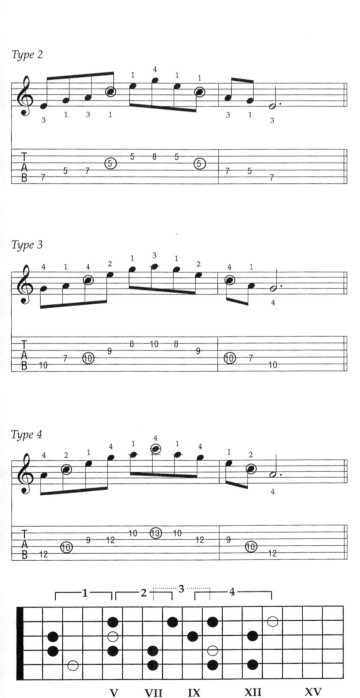

Cmaj7

C

Type 1

Type 2

Type 3

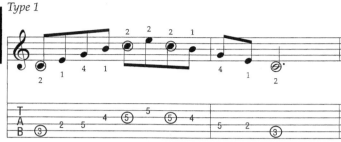

Type 4

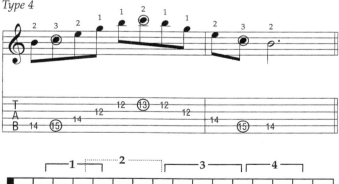

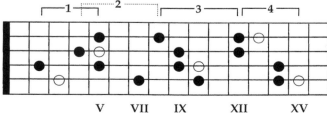

Cmaj9

Type 1

Type 2

Type 3

Type 4

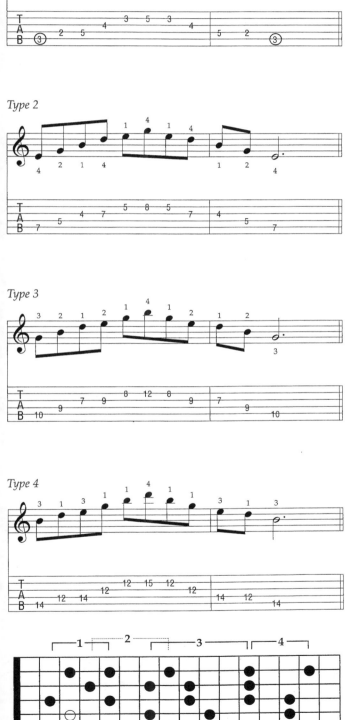

Cmaj9(#11)

Type 1

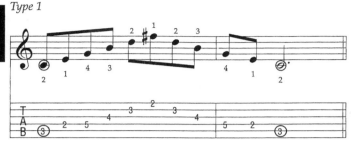

Type 2

Type 3

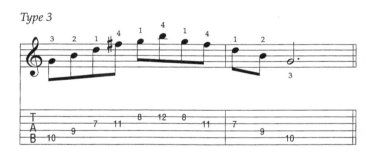

Type 4

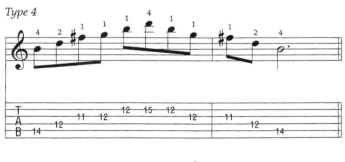

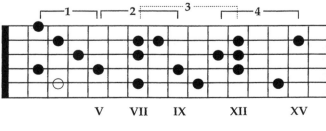

Cm

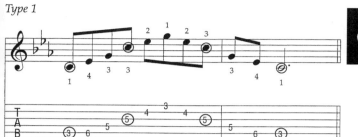

Type 1

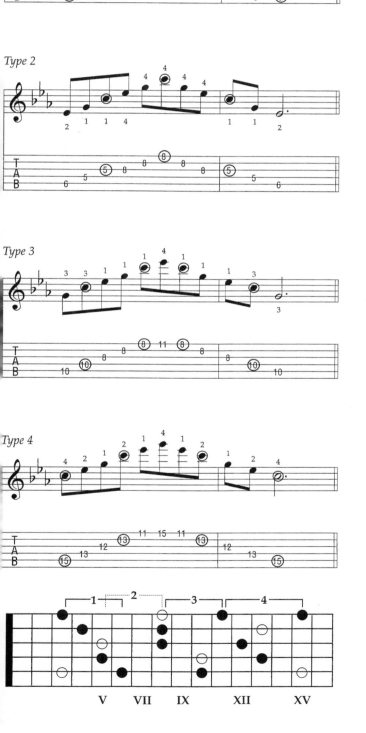

Type 2

Type 3

Type 4

Cm6

Type 1

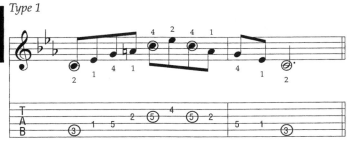

Type 2

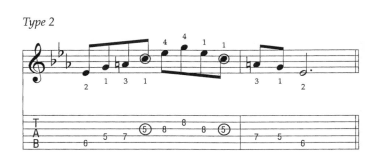

Type 3

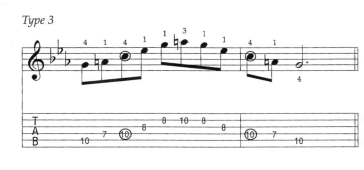

Type 4

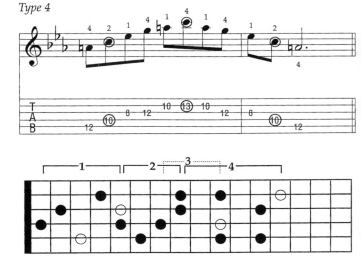

Cm7

Type 1

Type 2

Type 3

Type 4

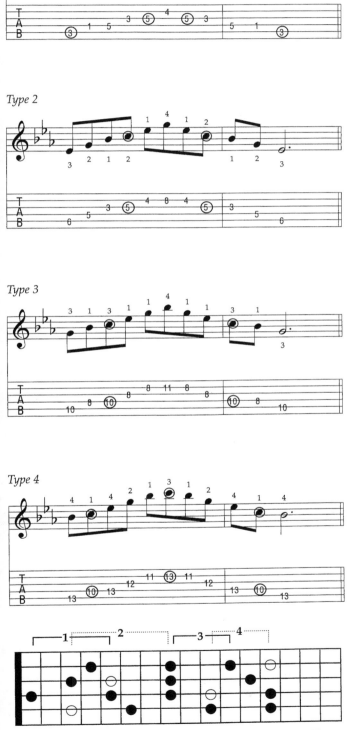

Cm9

C

Type 1

Type 2

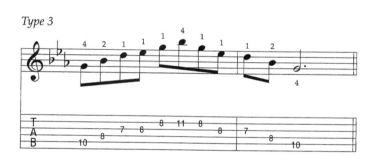

Type 3

Type 4

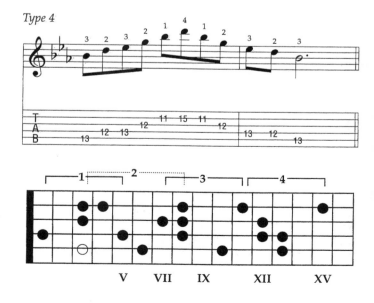

Cm11

Type 1

Type 2

Type 3

Type 4

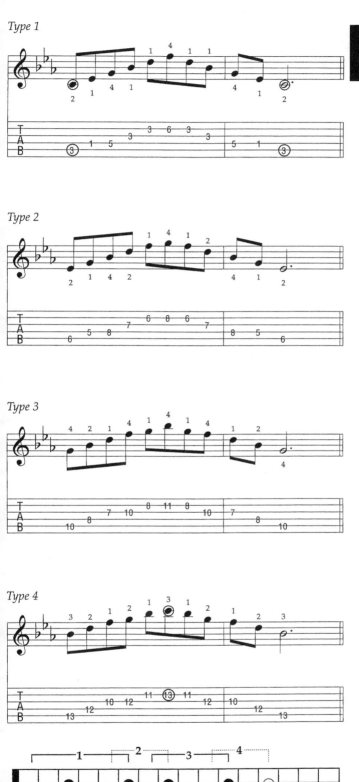

Cm(maj7)

Type 1

Type 2

Type 3

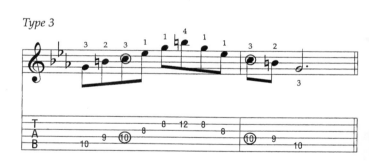

Type 4

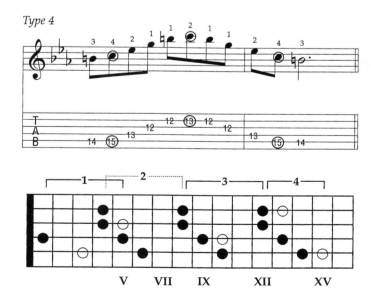

C7

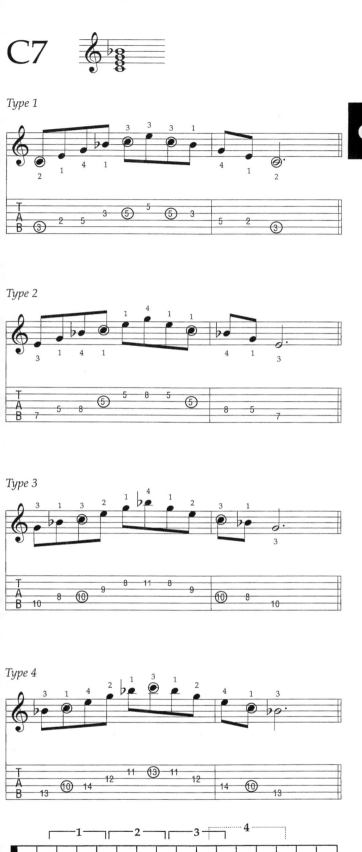

Type 1

Type 2

Type 3

Type 4

C

C9

Type 1

Type 2

Type 3

Type 4

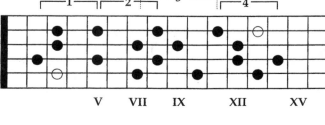

C7♭9

Type 1

Type 2

Type 3

Type 4

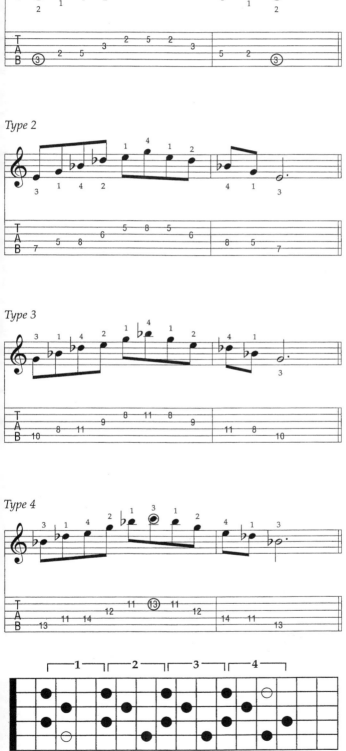

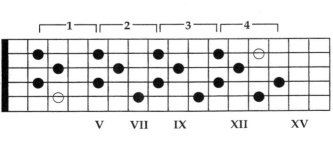

C7#9

Type 1

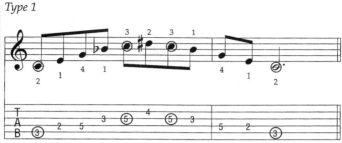

Type 2

Type 3

Type 4

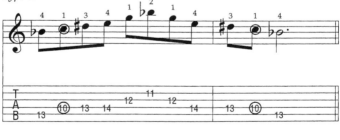

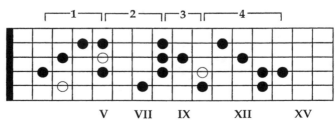

C9#11

Type 1

C

Type 2

Type 3

Type 4

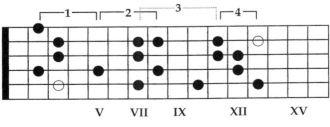

C7♭5

Type 1

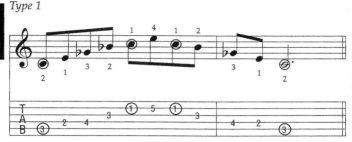

Type 2

Type 3

Type 4

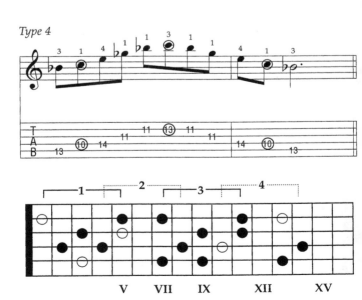

C7+

Type 1

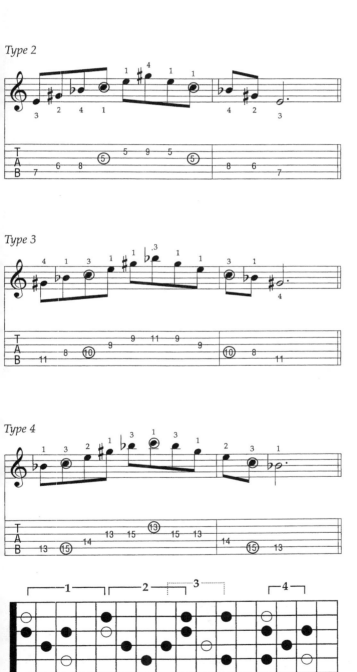

Type 2

Type 3

Type 4

Cm7♭5

Type 1

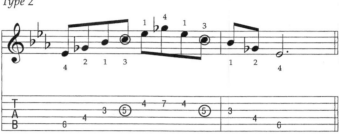

Type 2

Type 3

Type 4

C°7

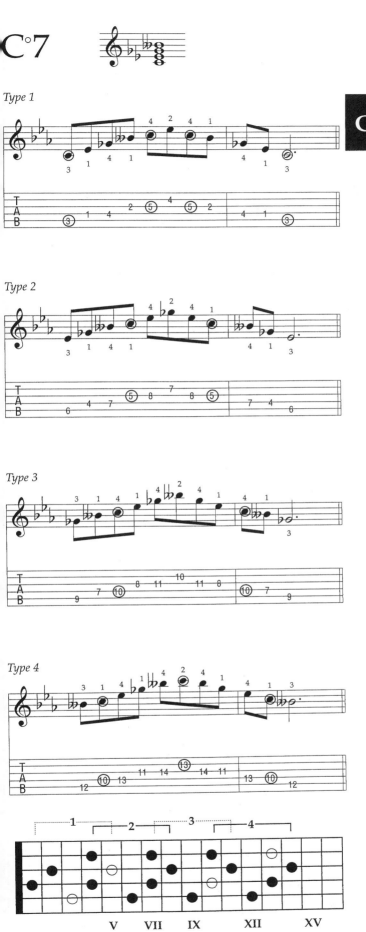

Type 1

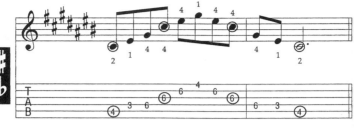

Type 2

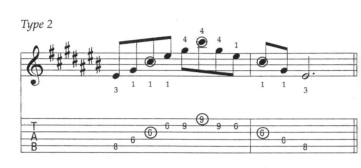

Type 3

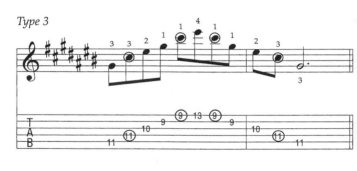

Type 4

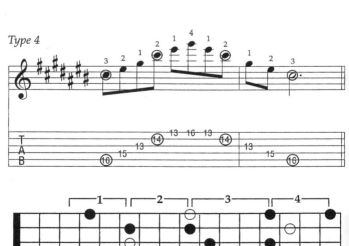

C#6

Type 1

Type 2

Type 3

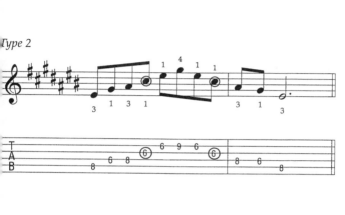

Type 4

C#maj7

Type 1

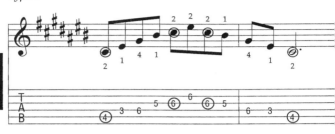

Type 2

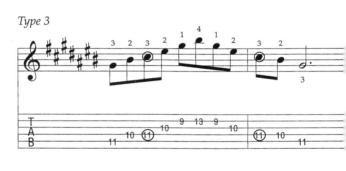

Type 3

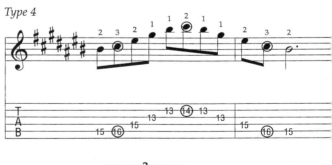

Type 4

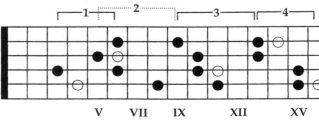

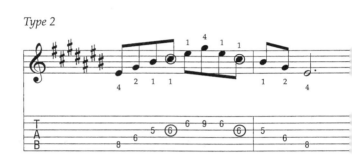

C#maj9

Type 1

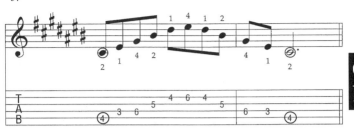

Type 2

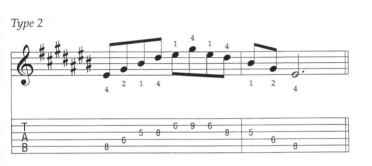

Type 3

Type 4

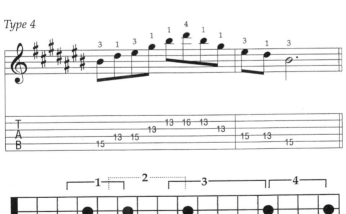

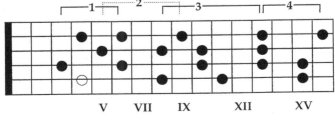

C♯maj9(♯11)

Type 1

Type 2

Type 3

Type 4

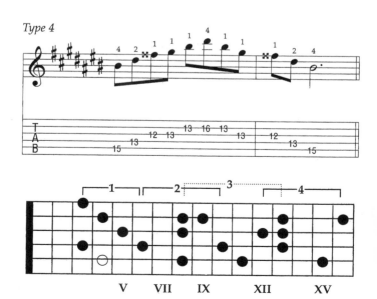

Type 1

Type 2

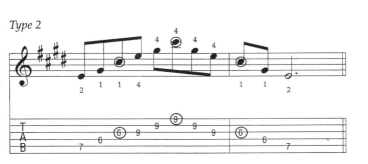

Type 3

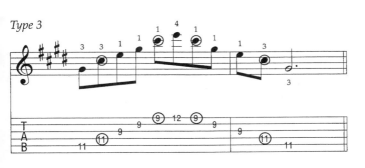

Type 4

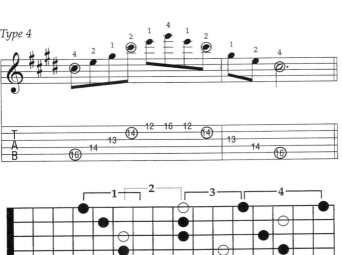

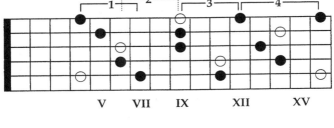

C#m6

Type 1

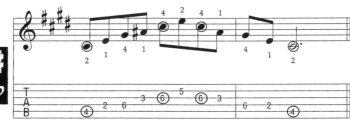

Type 2

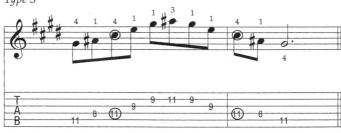

Type 3

Type 4

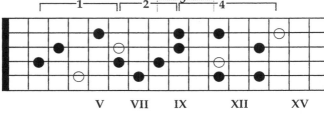

C#m7

Type 1

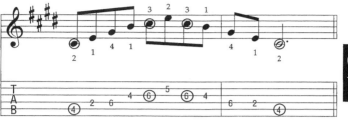

Type 2

Type 3

Type 4

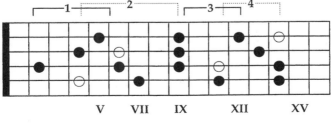

C#m9

Type 1

Type 2

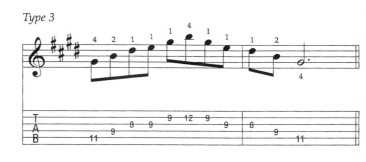

Type 3

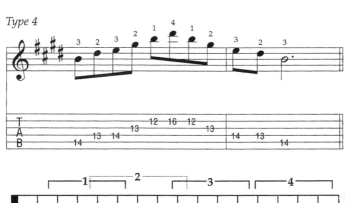

Type 4

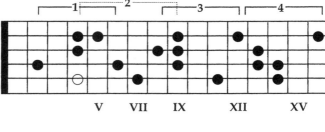

C#m11

Type 1

Type 2

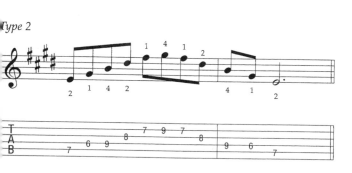

Type 3

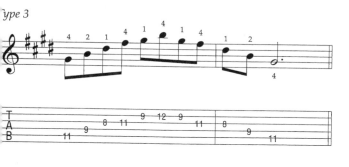

Type 4

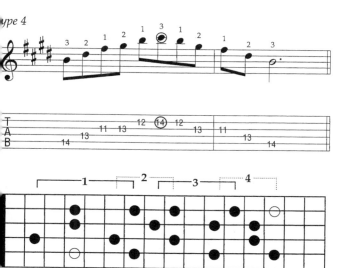

C#m(maj7)

Type 1

Type 2

Type 3

Type 4

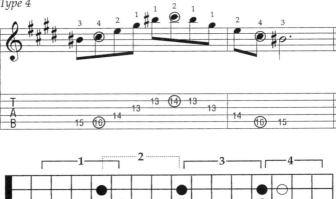

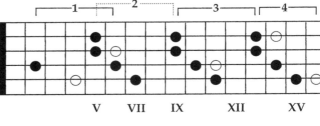

C#7

Type 1

Type 2

Type 3

Type 4

C#9

Type 1

Type 2

Type 3

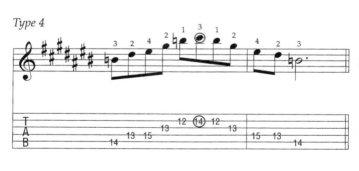

Type 4

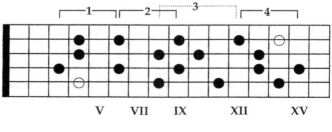

C#7♭9

C#
D♭

Type 1

Type 2

Type 3

Type 4

C#7#9

Type 1

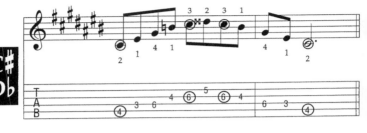

Type 2

Type 3

Type 4

**C#
D♭**

C#9#11

Type 1

Type 2

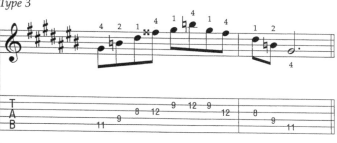

Type 3

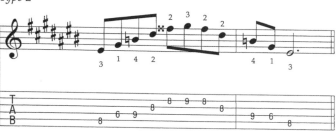

Type 4

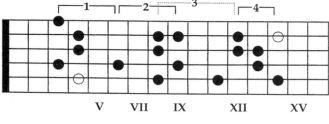

C#7b5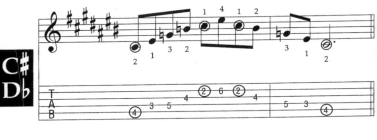

Type 1

Type 2

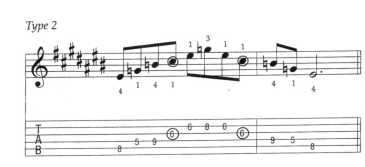

Type 3

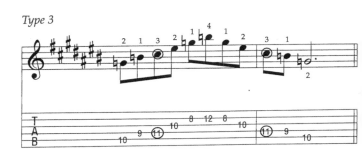

Type 4

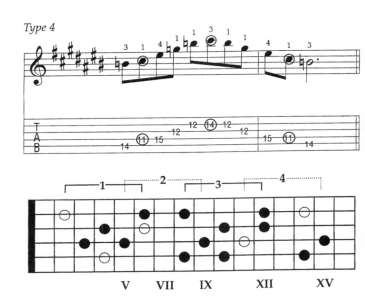

C#7+

Type 1

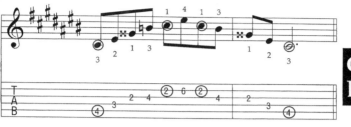

Type 2

Type 3

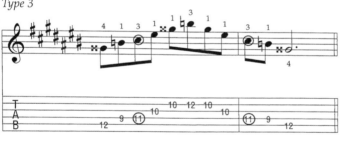

Type 4

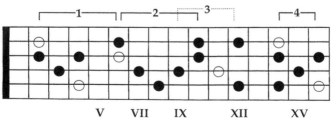

C#m7♭5

Type 1

Type 2

Type 3

Type 4

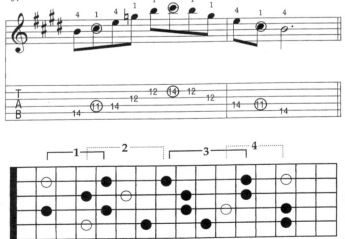

C#°7

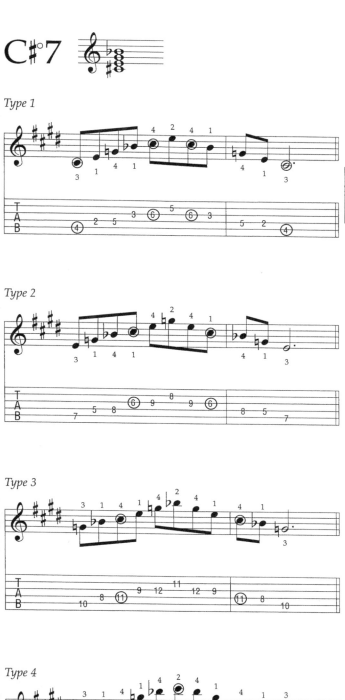

Type 1

Type 2

Type 3

Type 4

C#
Db

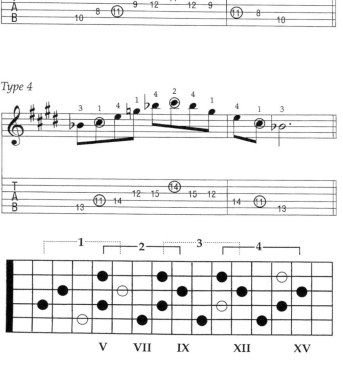

D

Type 1

Type 2

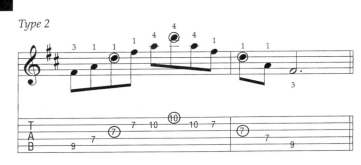

Type 3

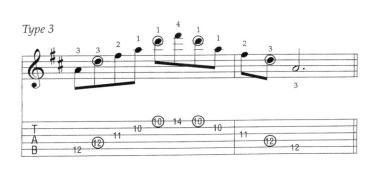

Type 4

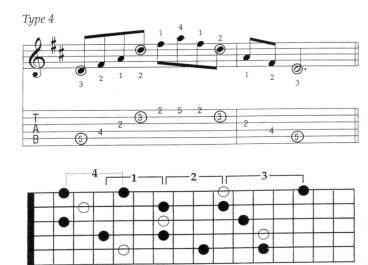

D6

Type 1

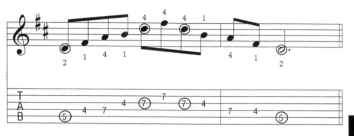

D

Type 2

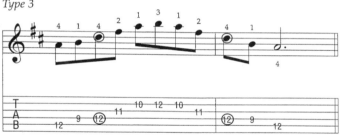

Type 3

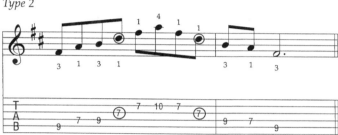

Type 4

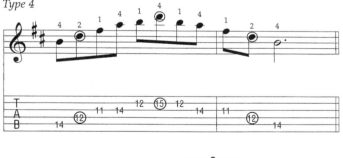

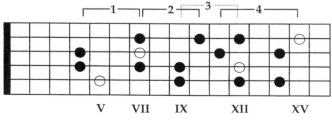

Dmaj7

Type 1

Type 2

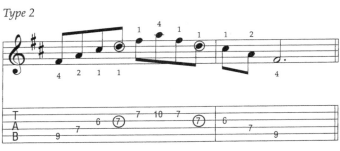

Type 3

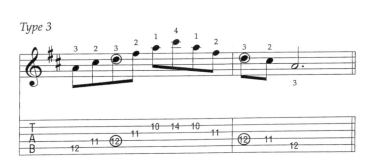

Type 4

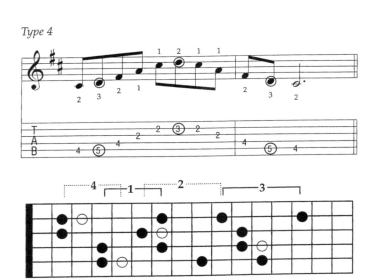

Dmaj9

Type 1

D

Type 2

Type 3

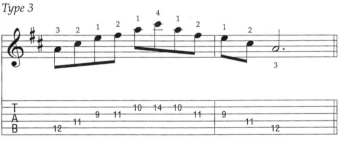

Type 4

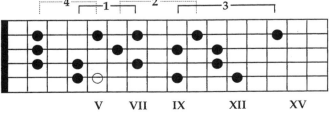

Dmaj9(#11)

Type 1

Type 2

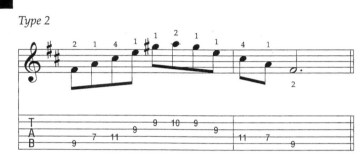

Type 3

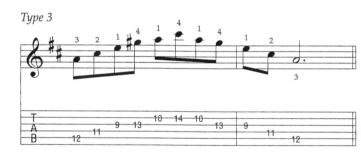

Type 4

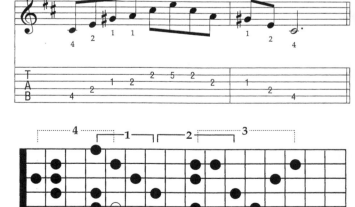

Dm

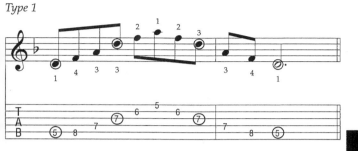

Type 1

D

Type 2

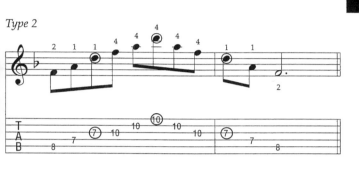

Type 3

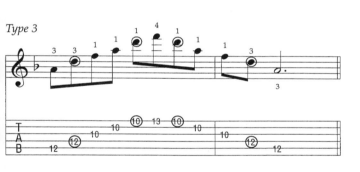

Type 4

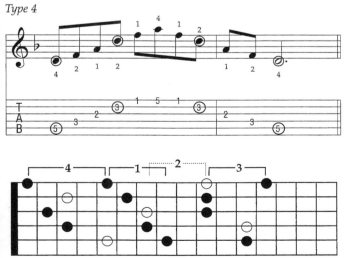

Dm6

Type 1

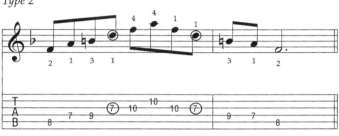

Type 2

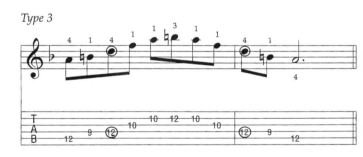

Type 3

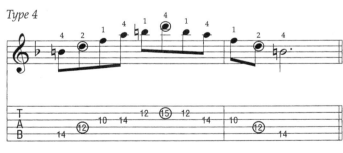

Type 4

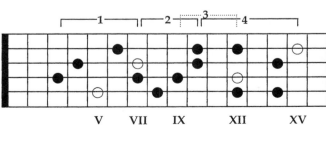

D

Dm7

D

Type 1

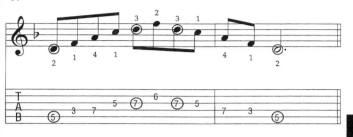

Type 2

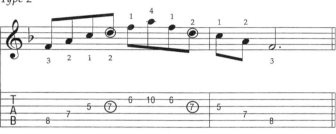

Type 3

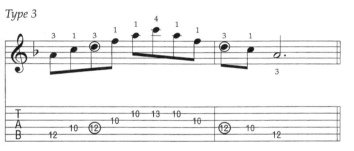

Type 4

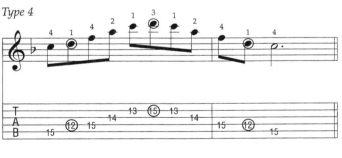

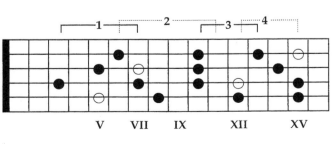

Dm9

Type 1

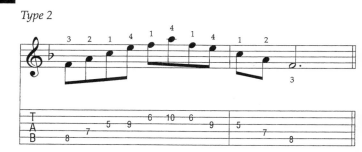

D

Type 2

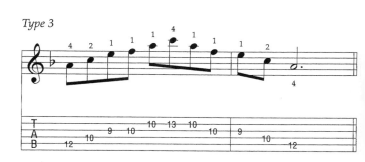

Type 3

Type 4

Dm11

Type 1

Type 2

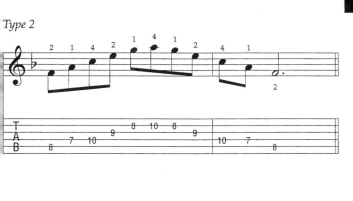

Type 3

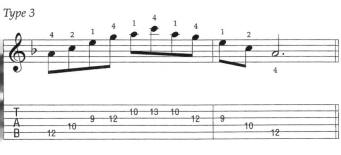

Type 4

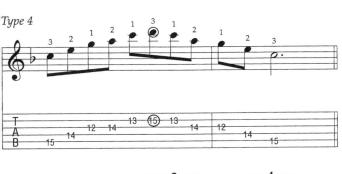

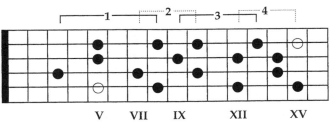

D

Dm(maj7)

Type 1

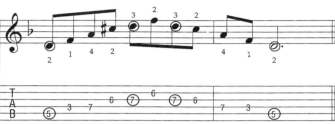

Type 2

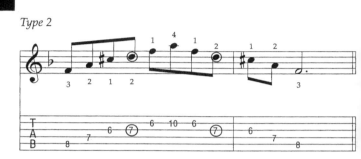

Type 3

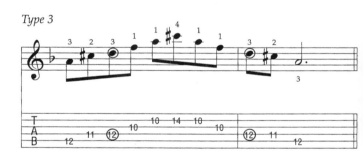

Type 4

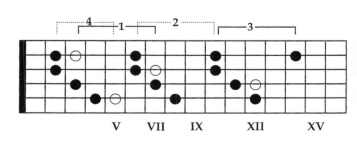

D7

Type 1

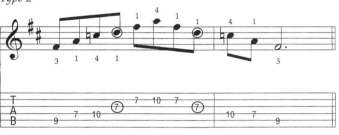

Type 2

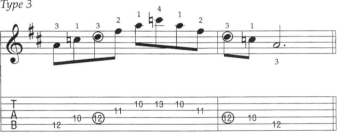

Type 3

Type 4

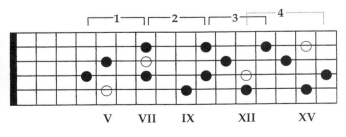

D9

Type 1

Type 2

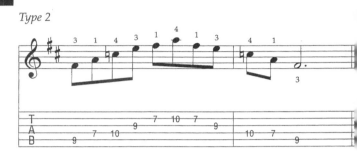

Type 3

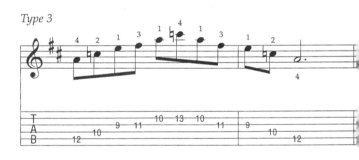

Type 4

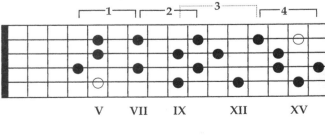

D7♭9

Type 1

D

Type 2

Type 3

Type 4

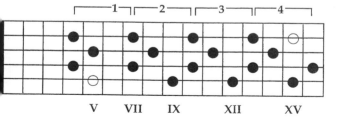

D7♯9

Type 1

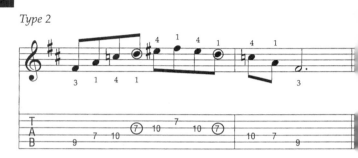

Type 2

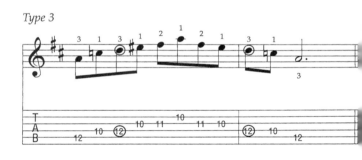

Type 3

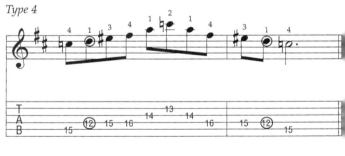

Type 4

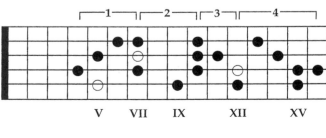

D9#11

Type 1

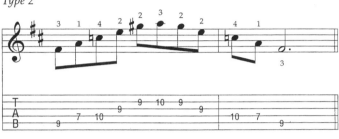

Type 2

Type 3

Type 4

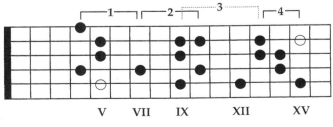

D

D7♭5

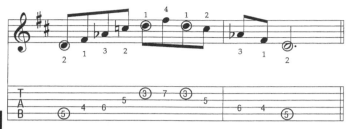

Type 1

D

Type 2

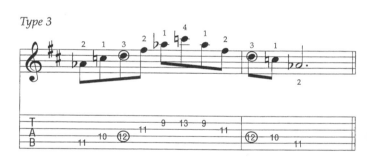

Type 3

Type 4

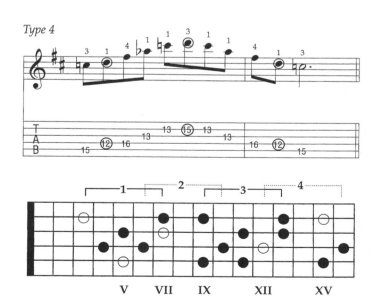

D7+

D

Type 1

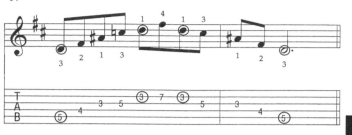

Type 2

Type 3

Type 4

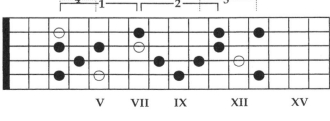

Dm7♭5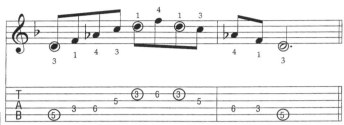

Type 1

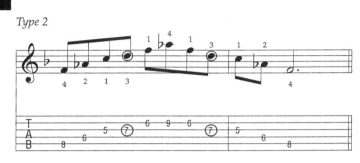

Type 2

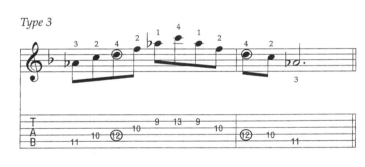

Type 3

Type 4

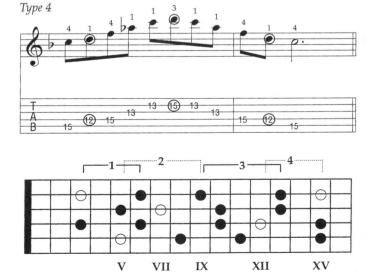

D°7

Type 1

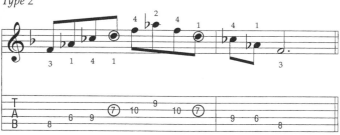

D

Type 2

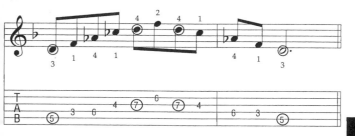

Type 3

Type 4

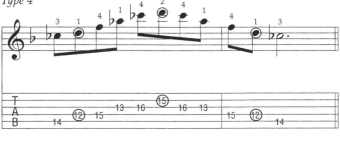

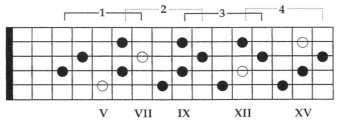

Type 1

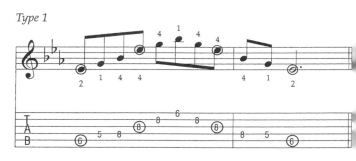

Type 2

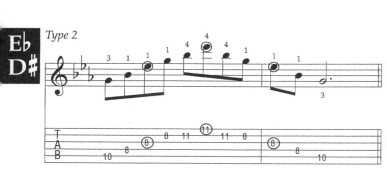

Type 3

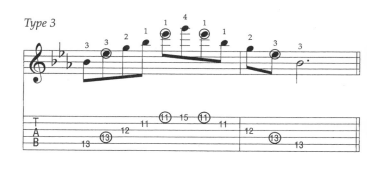

Type 4

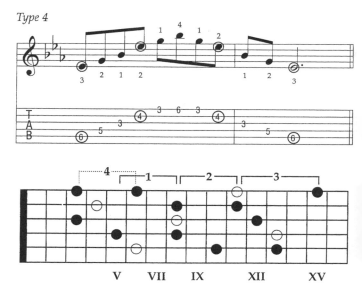

E♭6

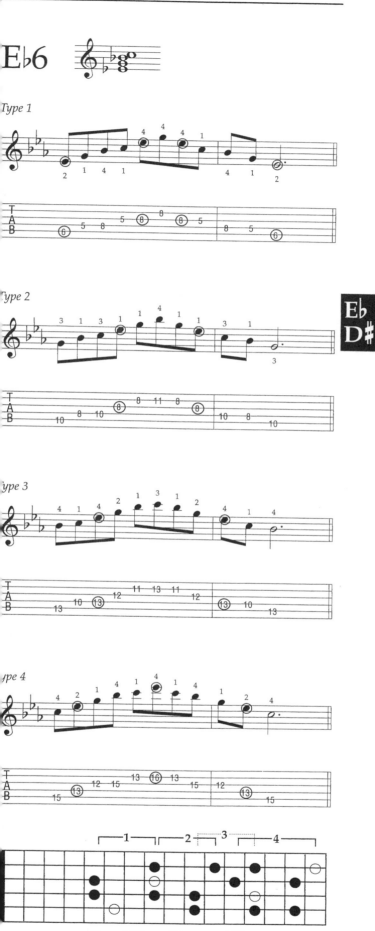

E♭maj7

Type 1

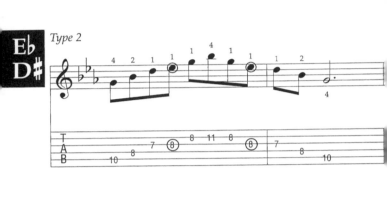

Type 2

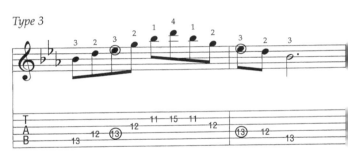

Type 3

Type 4

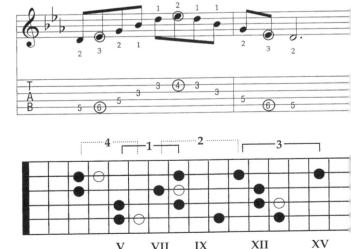

E♭maj9

Type 1

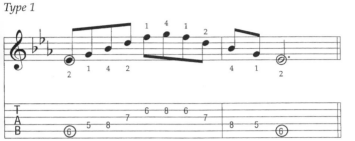

Type 2

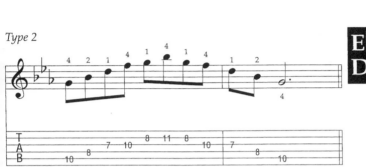

E♭ D♯

Type 3

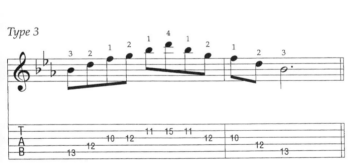

Type 4

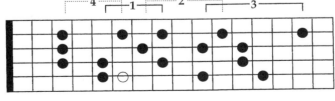

E♭maj9(♯11)

Type 1

Type 2

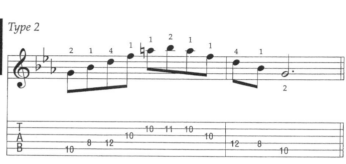

Type 3

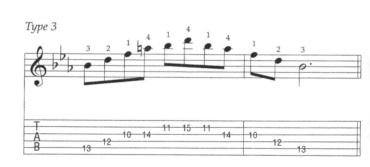

Type 4

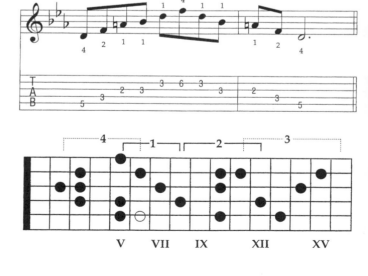

E♭m

Type 1

Type 2

E♭
D#

Type 3

Type 4

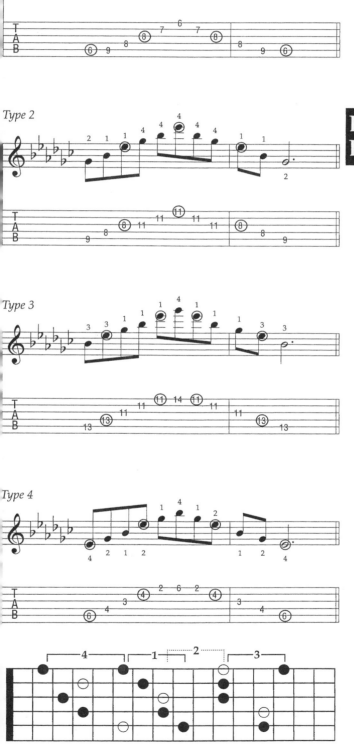

E♭m6

Type 1

Type 2

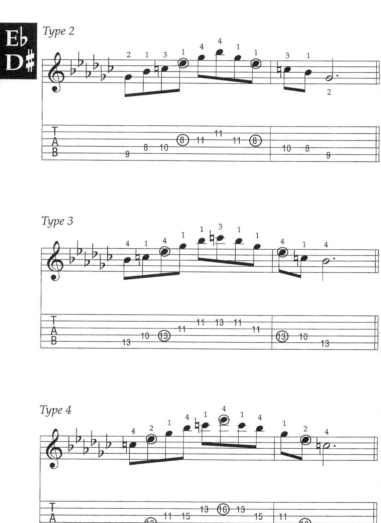

Type 3

Type 4

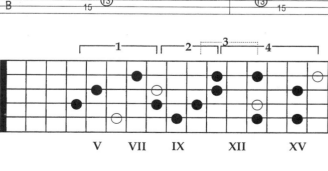

E♭m7

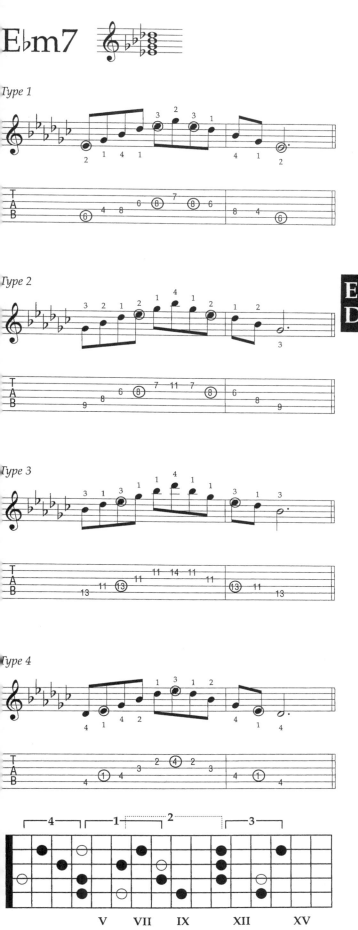

Type 1

Type 2

Type 3

Type 4

Ebm9

Type 1

Type 2

Type 3

Type 4

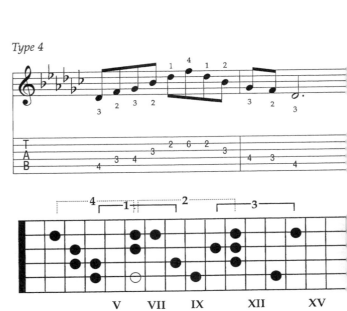

E♭m11

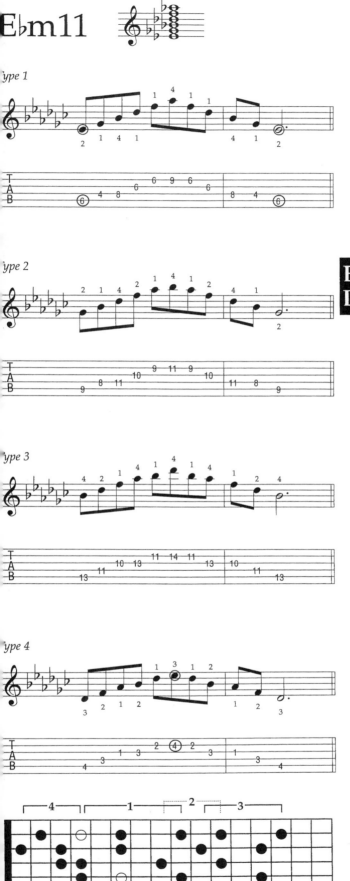

Type 1

Type 2

Type 3

Type 4

E♭m(maj7)

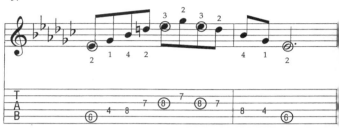

Type 1

Type 2

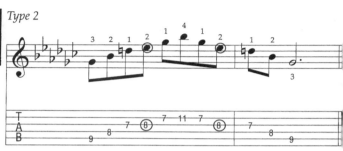

Type 3

Type 4

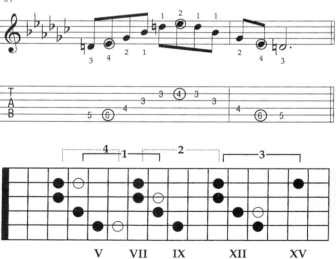

E♭7

Type 1

Type 2

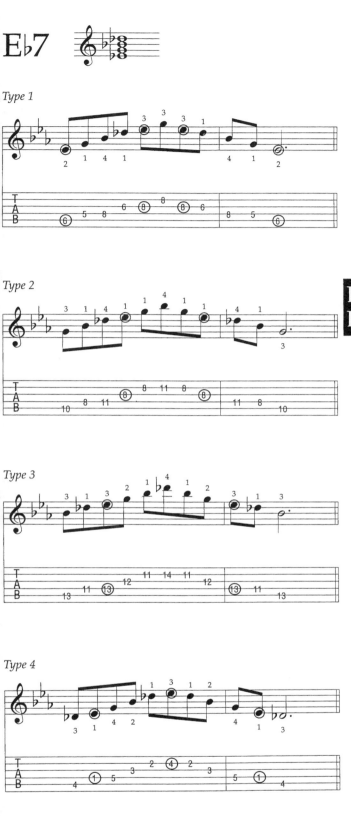

Type 3

Type 4

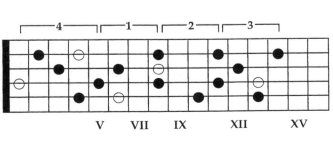

E♭9

Type 1

Type 2

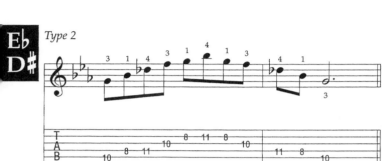

Type 3

Type 4

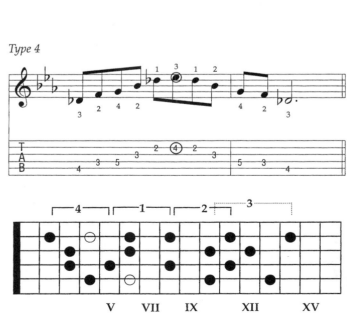

Eb7b9

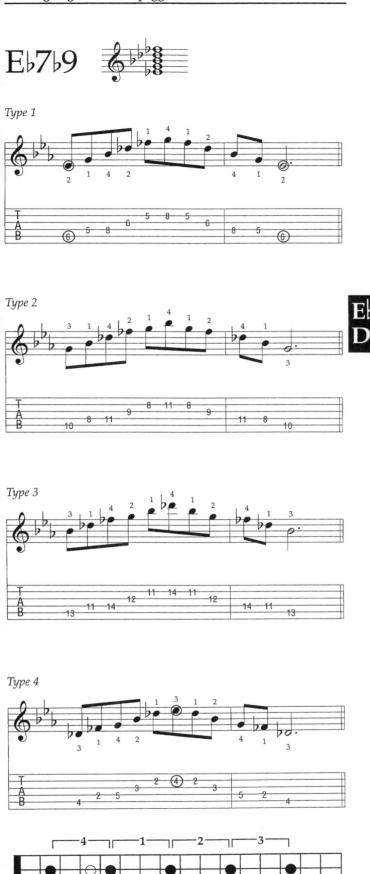

Type 1

Type 2

Eb
D#

Type 3

Type 4

E♭7♯9

Type 1

Type 2

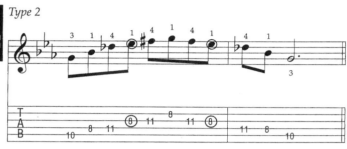

Type 3

Type 4

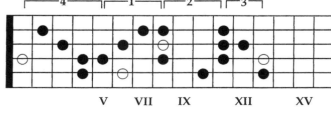

E♭9♯11

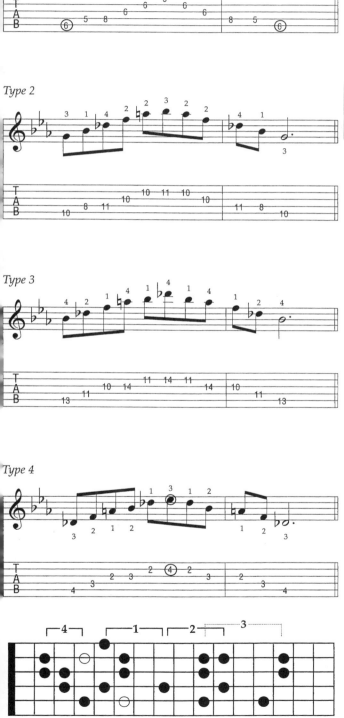

E♭7♭5

Type 1

Type 2

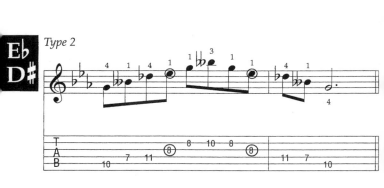

Type 3

Type 4

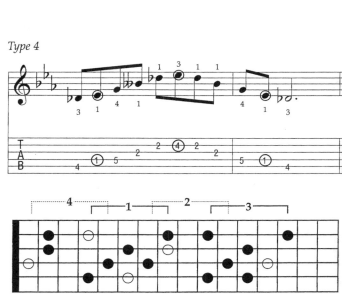

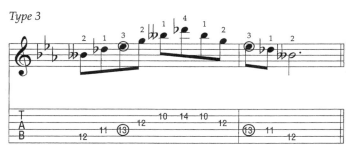

Type 1

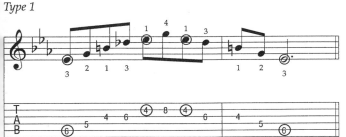

Type 2

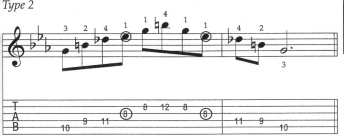

Type 3

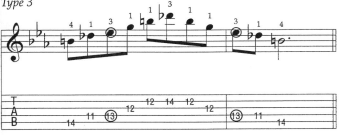

Type 4

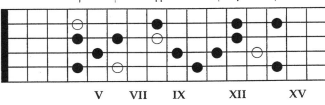

E♭m7♭5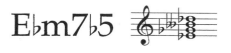

Type 1

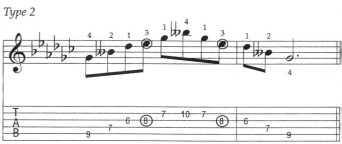

Type 2

Type 3

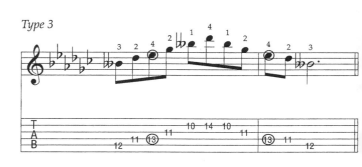

Type 4

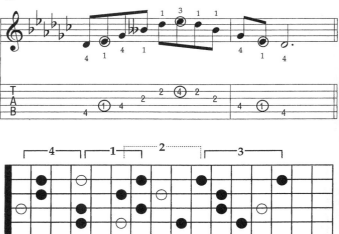

E♭°7

Type 1

Type 2

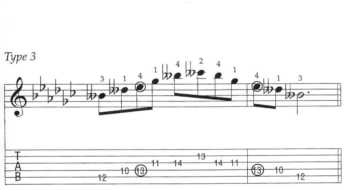

Type 3

Type 4

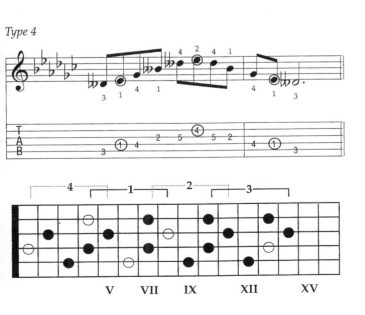

Type 1

Type 2

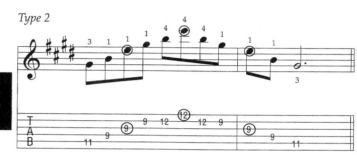

E

Type 3

Type 4

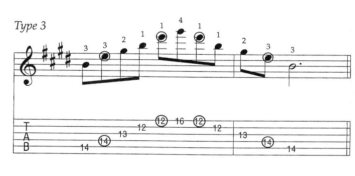

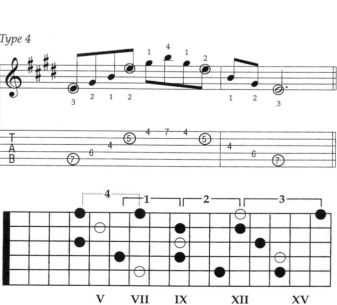

E6

Type 1

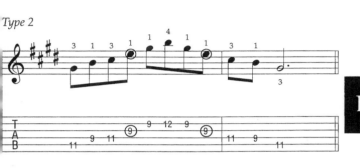

Type 2

E

Type 3

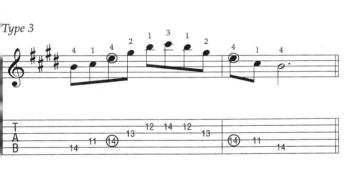

Type 4

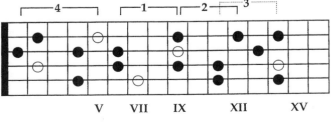

Emaj7

Type 1

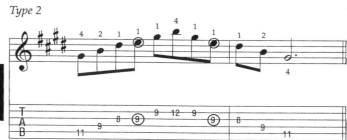

Type 2

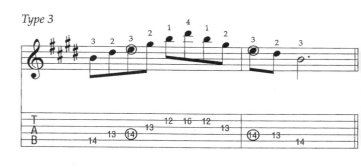

Type 3

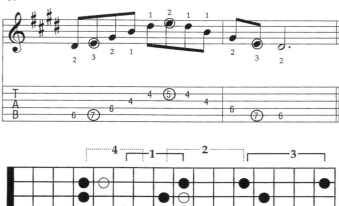

Type 4

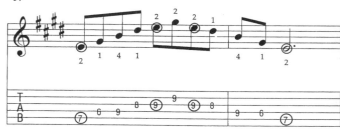

Emaj9

Type 1

Type 2

Type 3

Type 4

Emaj9(♯11)

Type 1

Type 2

Type 3

Type 4

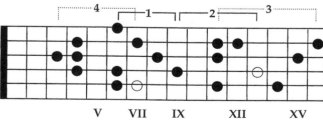

Em

Type 1

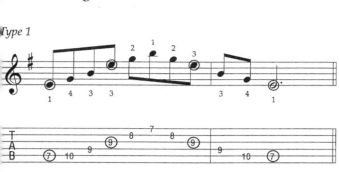

Type 2

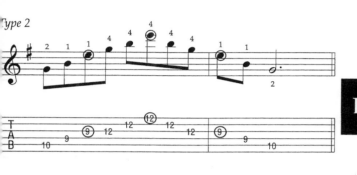

E

Type 3

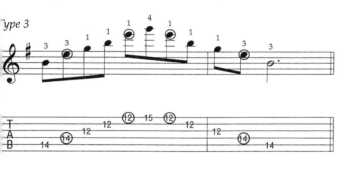

Type 4

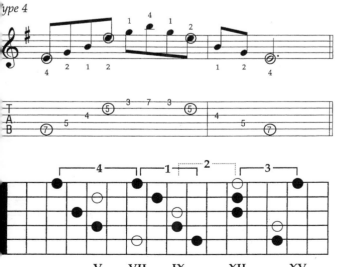

Em6

Type 1

Type 2

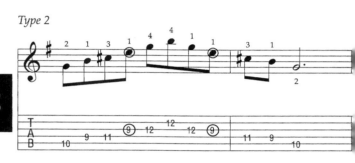

Type 3

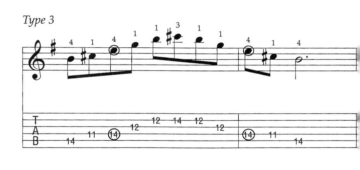

Type 4

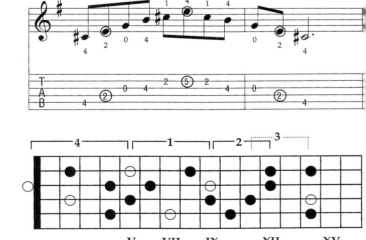

Em7

Type 1

Type 2

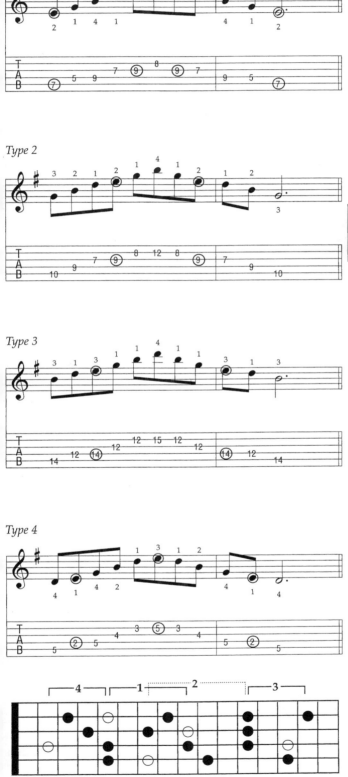

Type 3

Type 4

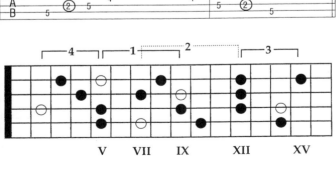

Em9

Type 1

Type 2

Type 3

Type 4

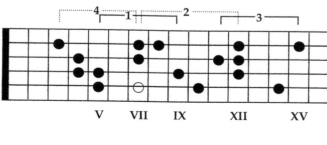

Em11

Type 1

Type 2

E

Type 3

Type 4

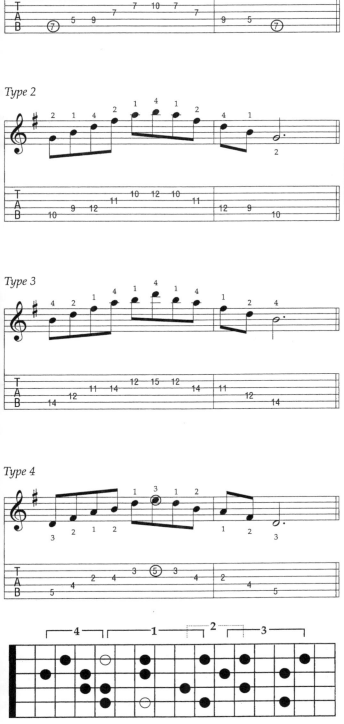

Em(maj7)

Type 1

Type 2

E

Type 3

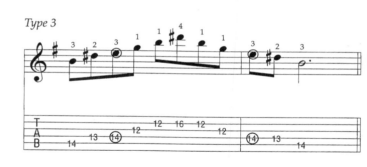

Type 4

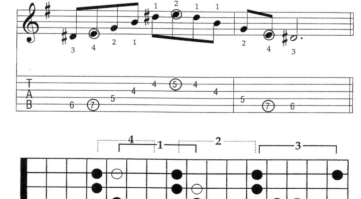

E7

Type 1

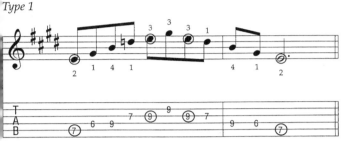

Type 2

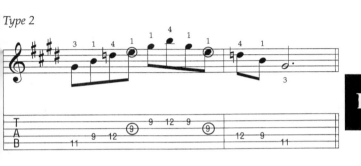

E

Type 3

Type 4

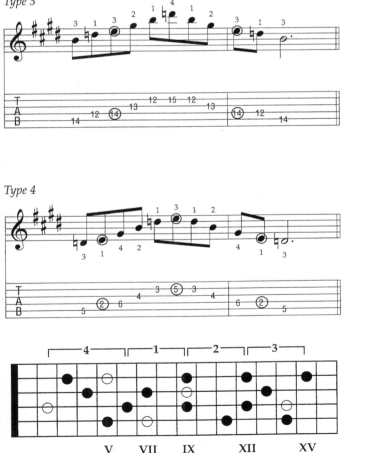

E9

Type 1

Type 2

Type 3

Type 4

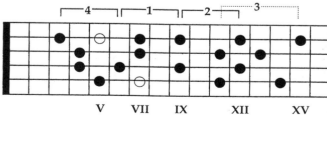

E7♭9

Type 1

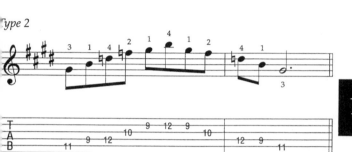

Type 2

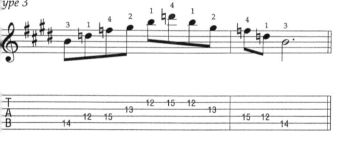

E

Type 3

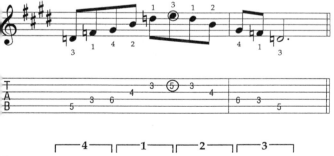

Type 4

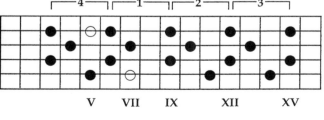

E7♯9

Type 1

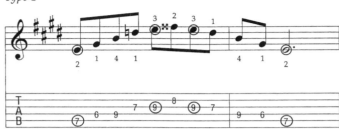

Type 2

Type 3

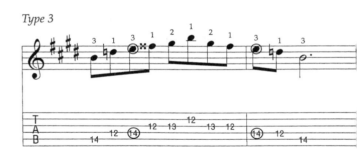

Type 4

E9♯11

Type 1

Type 2

E

Type 3

Type 4

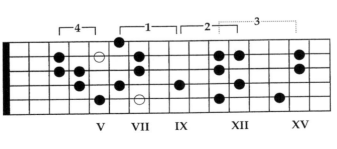

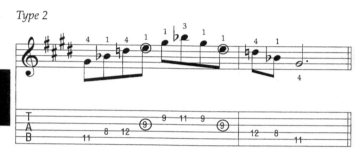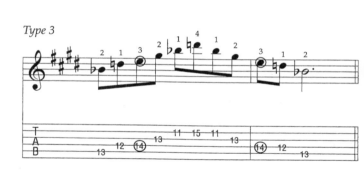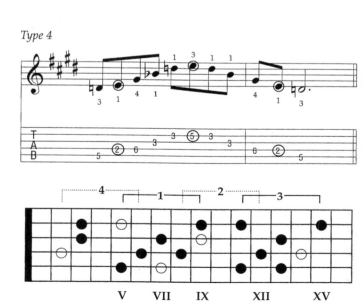

E7♭5

Type 1

Type 2

Type 3

Type 4

E7+

Type 1

Type 2

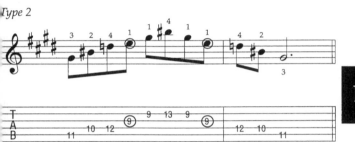

Type 3

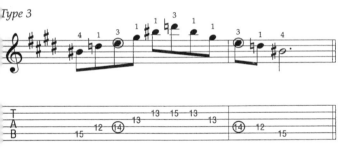

Type 4

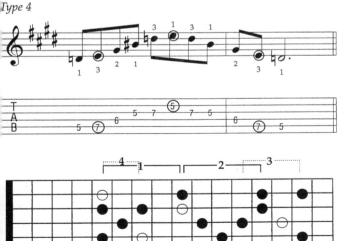

Em7♭5

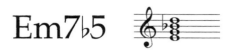

Type 1

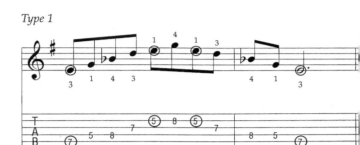

Type 2

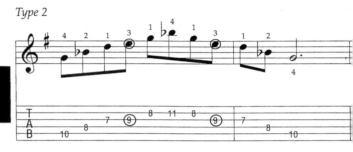

Type 3

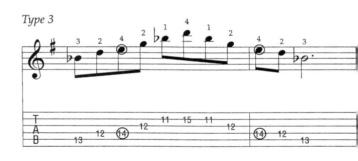

Type 4

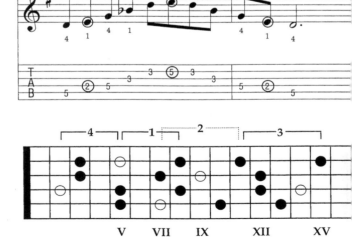

E°7

Type 1

Type 2

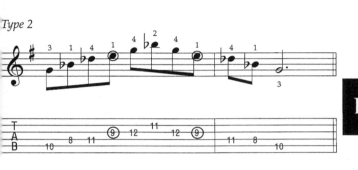

E

Type 3

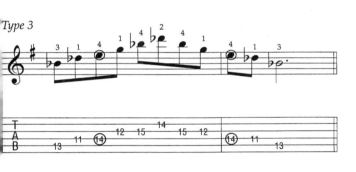

Type 4

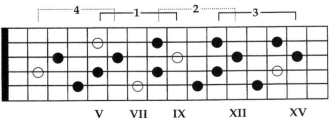

Type 1

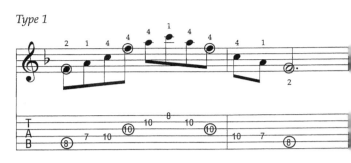

Type 2

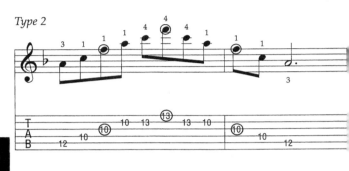

Type 3

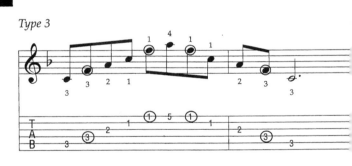

Type 4

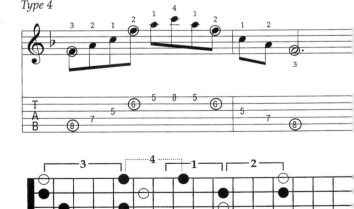

F6

Type 1

Type 2

Type 3

Type 4

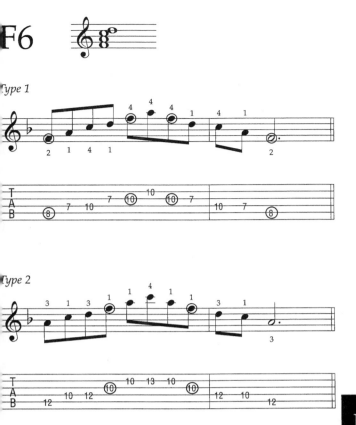

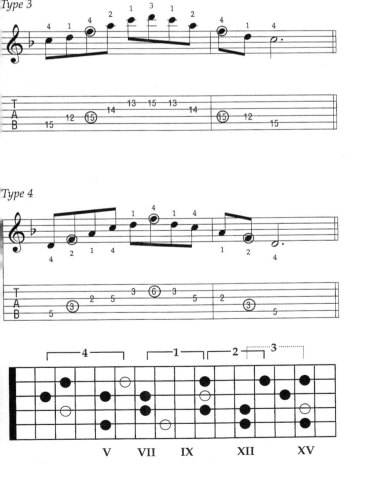

F

Fmaj7

Type 1

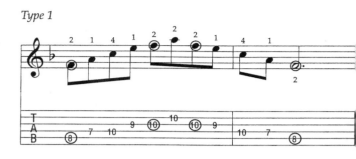

Type 2

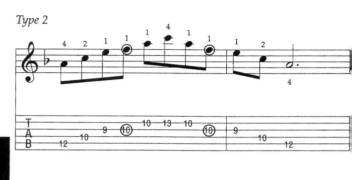

F

Type 3

Type 4

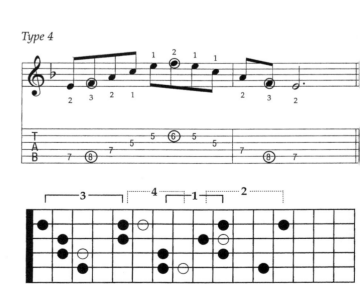

Fmaj9

Type 1

Type 2

Type 3

Type 4

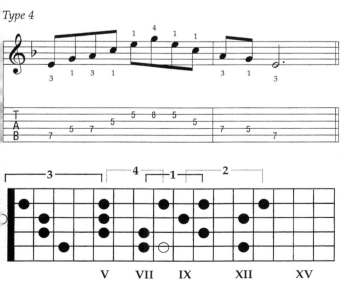

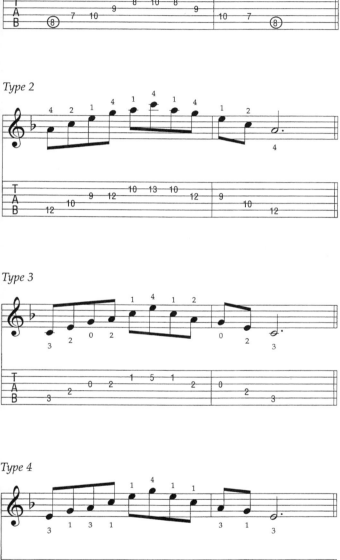

Fmaj9(♯11)

Type 1

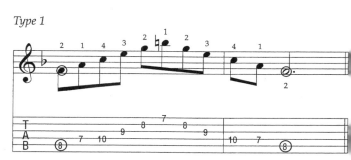

Type 2

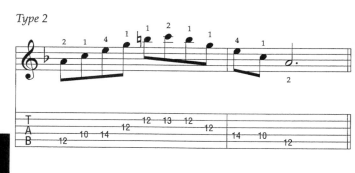

Type 3

Type 4

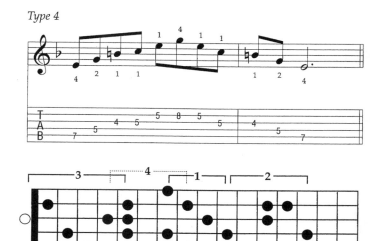

Fm

Type 1

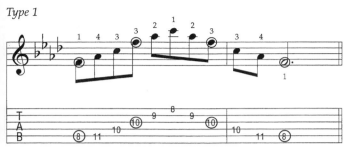

Type 2

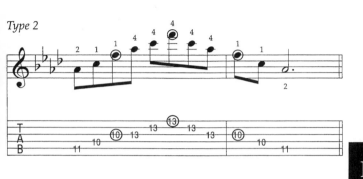

F

Type 3

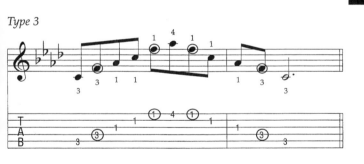

Type 4

Fm6

Type 1

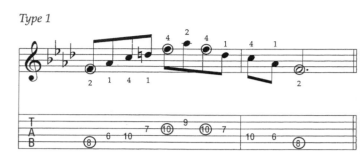

Type 2

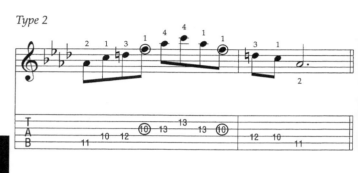

Type 3

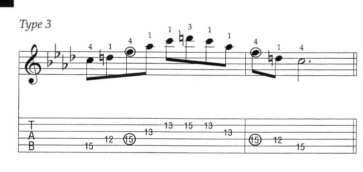

Type 4

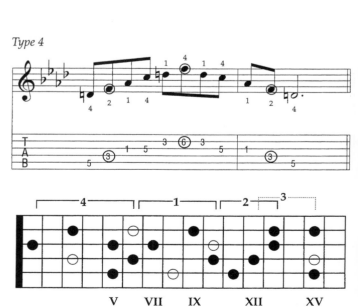

Fm7

Type 1

Type 2

F

Type 3

Type 4

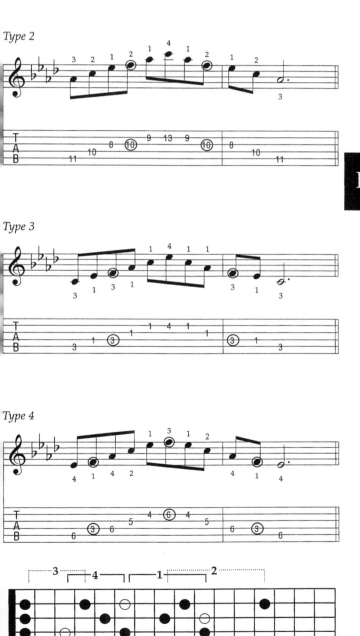

Fm9

Type 1

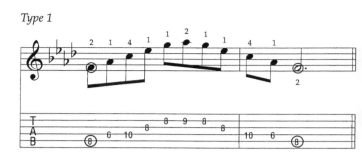

Type 2

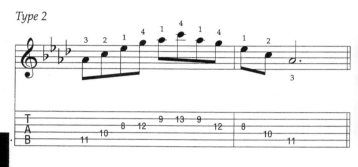

Type 3

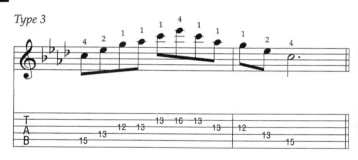

Type 4

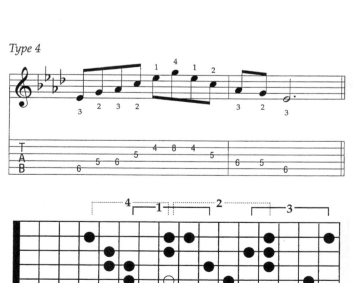

Fm11

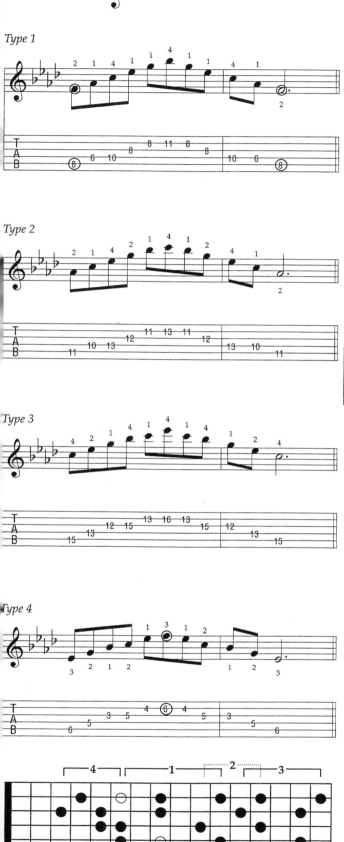

Type 1

Type 2

F

Type 3

Type 4

Fm(maj7)

Type 1

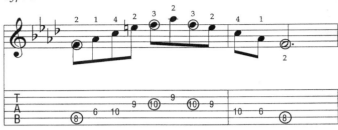

Type 2

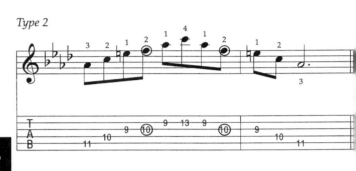

Type 3

Type 4

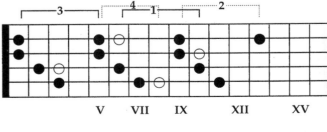

F7

Type 1

Type 2

F

Type 3

Type 4

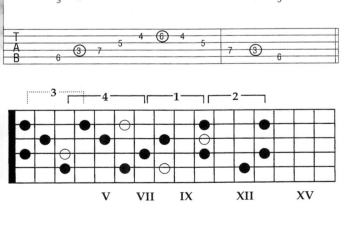

F9

Type 1

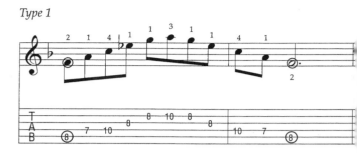

Type 2

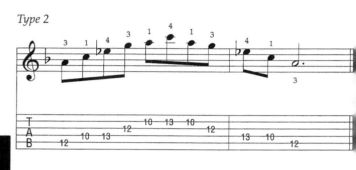

Type 3

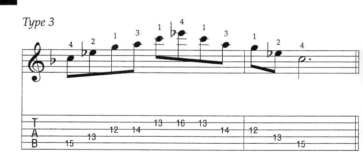

Type 4

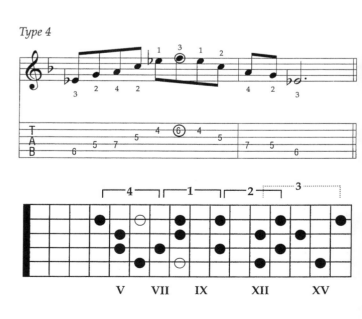

F

F7♭9

Type 1

Type 2

Type 3

Type 4

F

F7♯9

Type 1

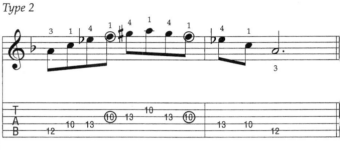

Type 2

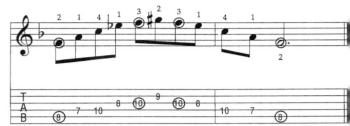

Type 3

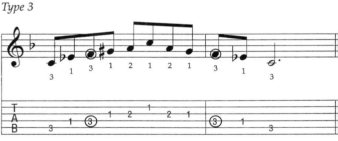

Type 4

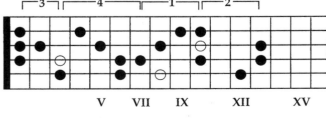

F9#11

Type 1

Type 2

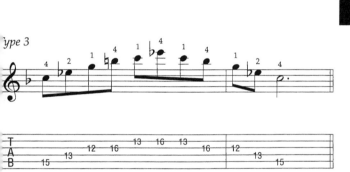

F

Type 3

Type 4

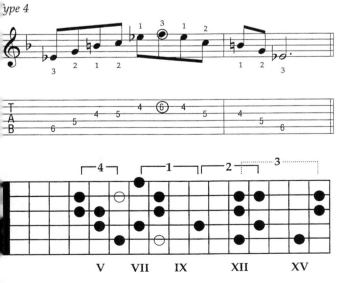

F7♭5

Type 1

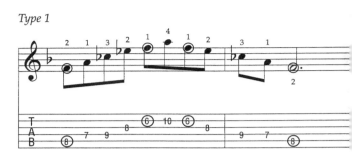

Type 2

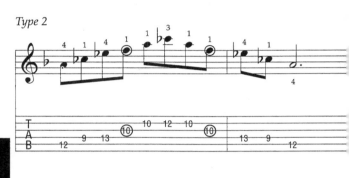

Type 3

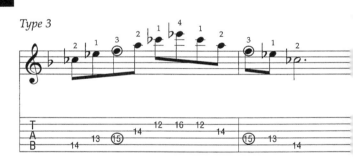

Type 4

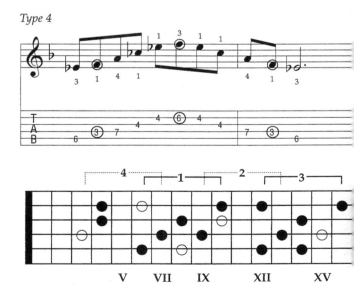

F7+

Type 1

Type 2

Type 3

Type 4

F

Fm7♭5

Type 1

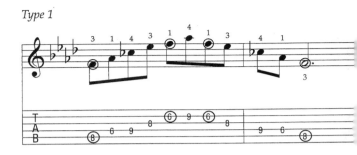

Type 2

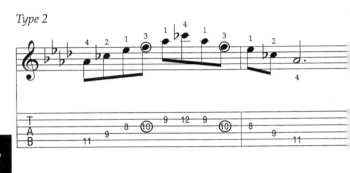

Type 3

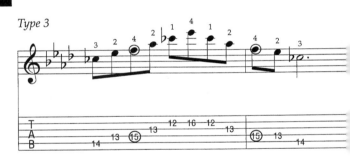

Type 4

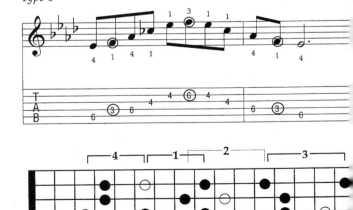

F°7

Type 1

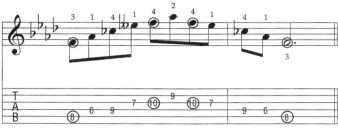

Type 2

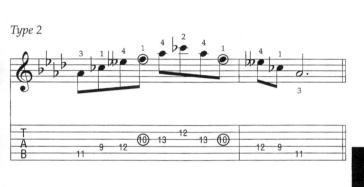

Type 3

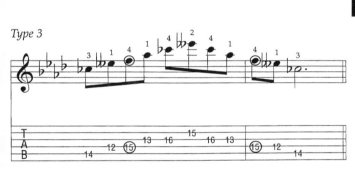

Type 4

F

Type 1

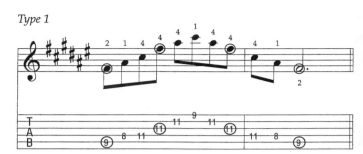

Type 2

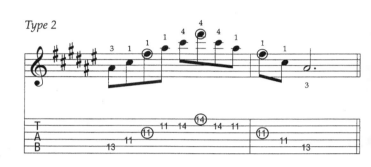

Type 3

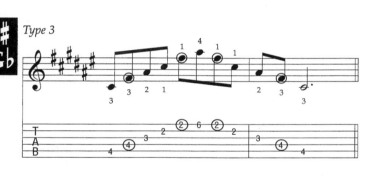

Type 4

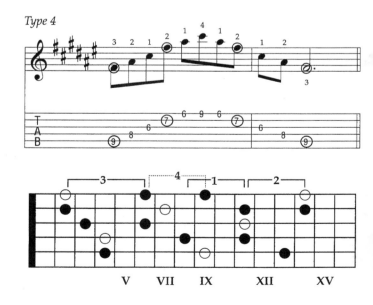

F#6

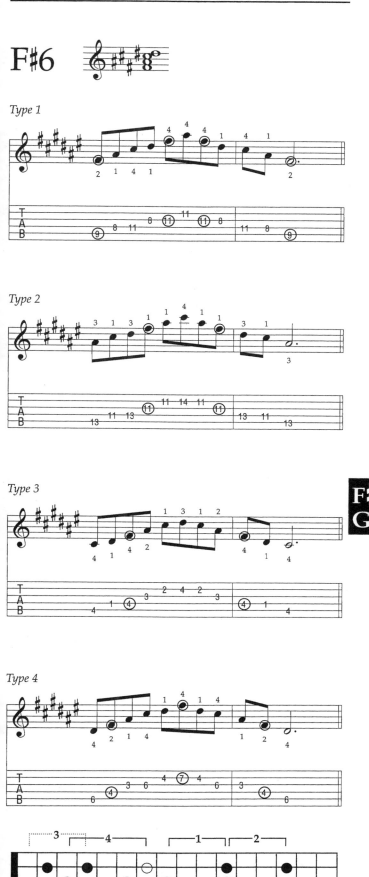

Type 1

Type 2

Type 3

F#
Gb

Type 4

F♯maj7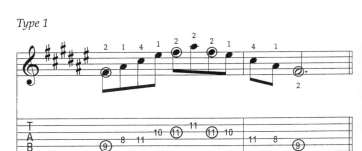

Type 1

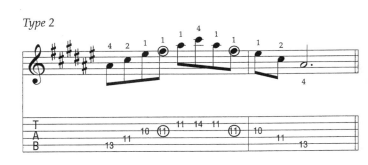

Type 2

Type 3

Type 4

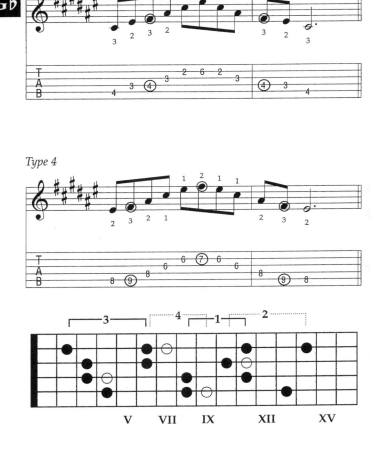

F#maj9

Type 1

Type 2

Type 3

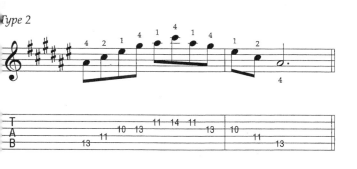

Type 4

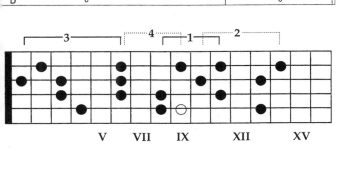

F#maj9(#11)

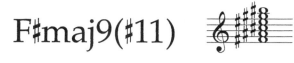

Type 1

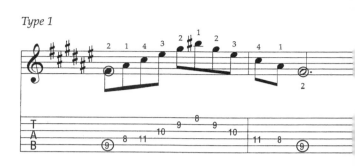

Type 2

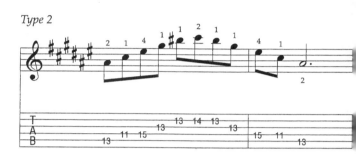

Type 3

Type 4

F#m

Type 1

Type 2

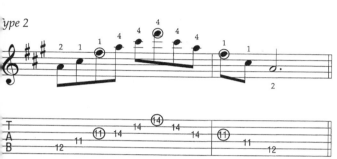

Type 3

F#
Gb

Type 4

F#m6

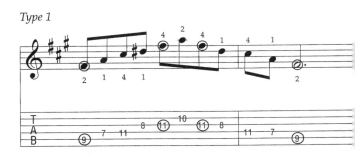

Type 1

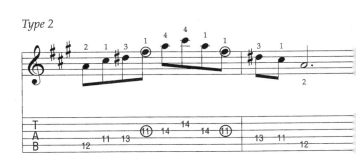

Type 2

Type 3

F#
Gb

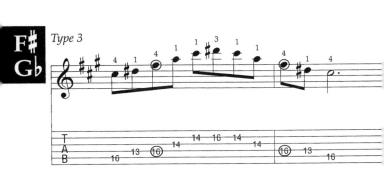

Type 4

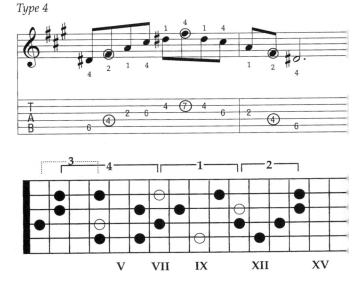

F#m7

Type 1

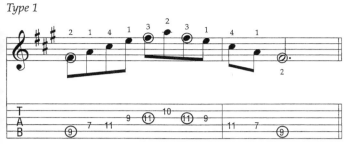

Type 2

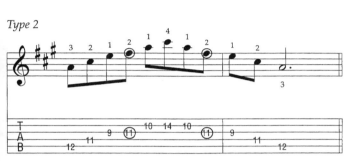

Type 3

Type 4

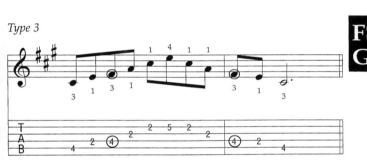

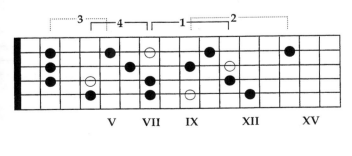

F♯m9

Type 1

Type 2

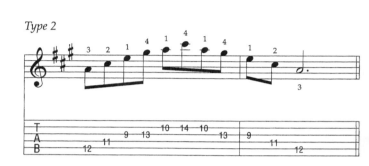

Type 3

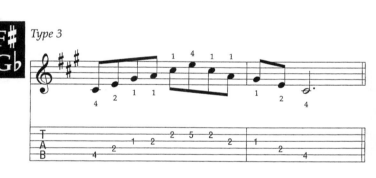

Type 4

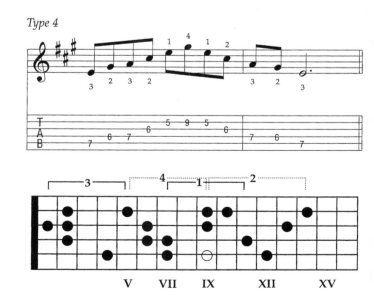

F#m11

Type 1

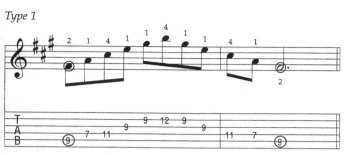

Type 2

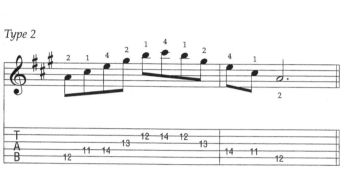

Type 3

Type 4

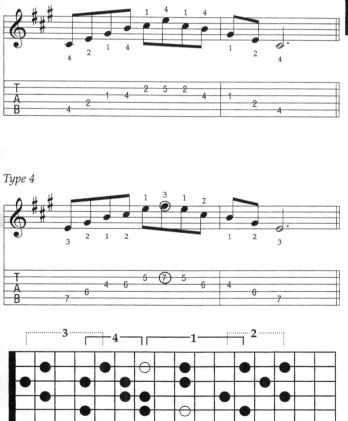

F#m(maj7)

Type 1

Type 2

Type 3

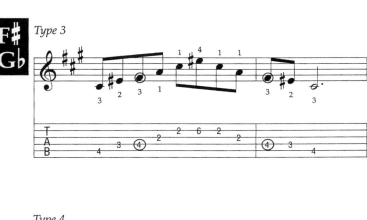

Type 4

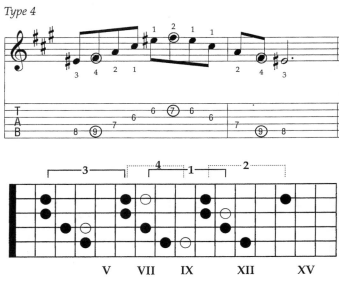

F#7

Type 1

Type 2

Type 3

Type 4

F♯9

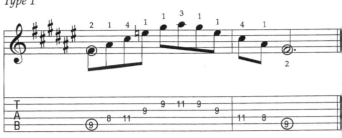

Type 1

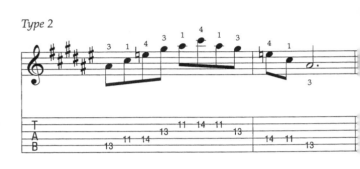

Type 2

Type 3

Type 4

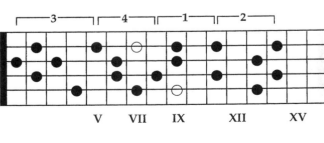

F♯
G♭

F#7♭9

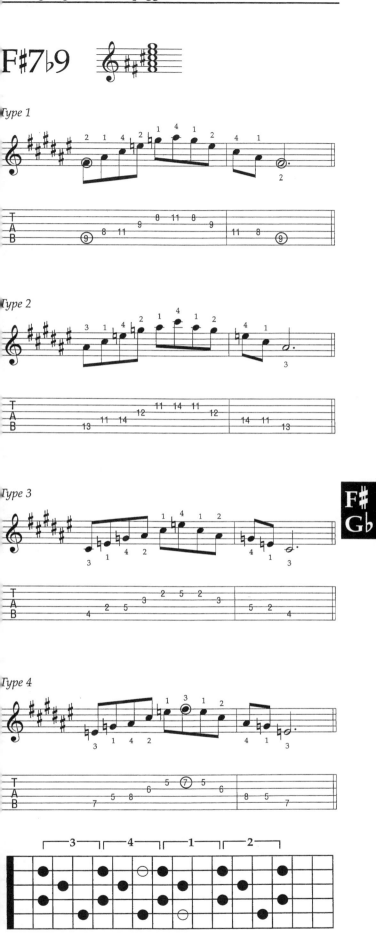

F♯7♯9

Type 1

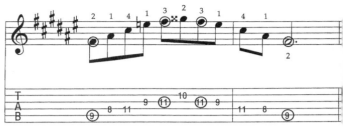

Type 2

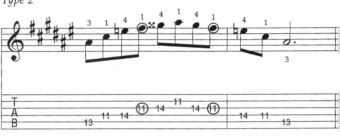

Type 3

Type 4

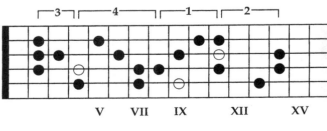

F#9#11

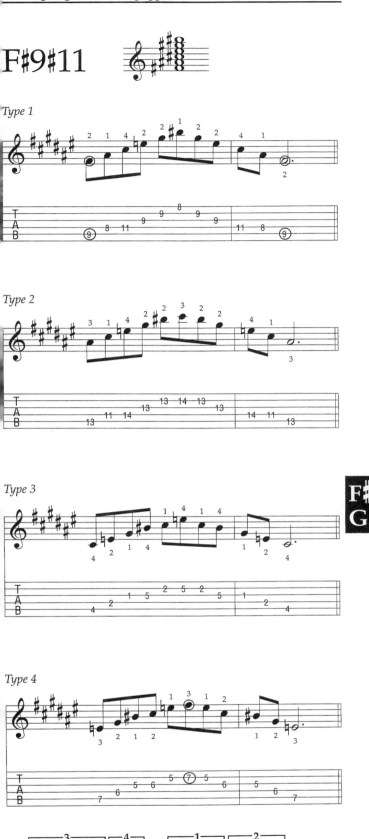

F#7♭5

Type 1

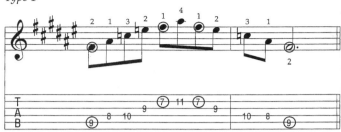

Type 2

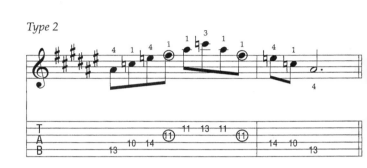

Type 3

Type 4

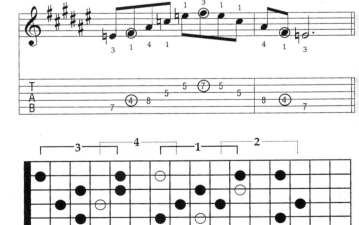

V   VII   IX   XII   XV

F#7+

Type 1

Type 2

Type 3

Type 4

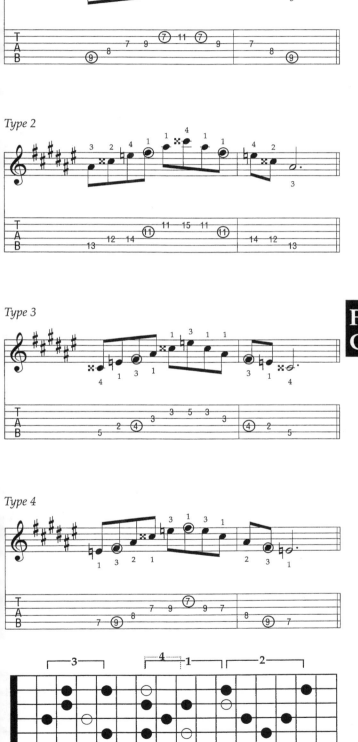

F♯m7♭5

Type 1

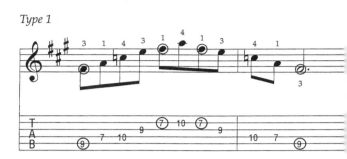

Type 2

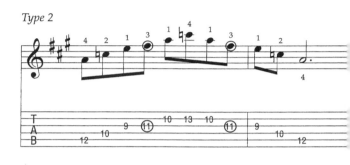

Type 3

Type 4

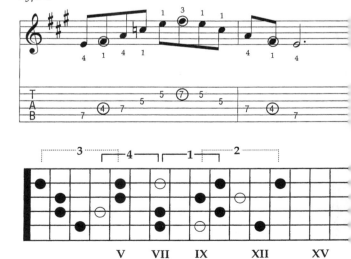

F#°7

Type 1

Type 2

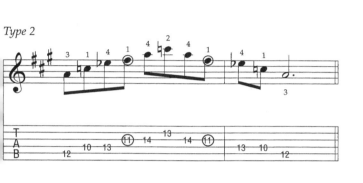

Type 3

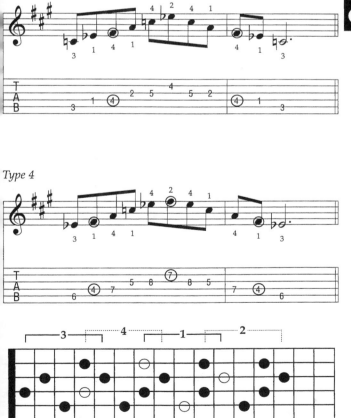

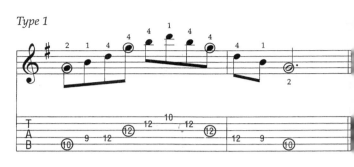

Type 1

Type 2

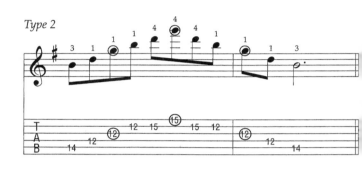

Type 3

G

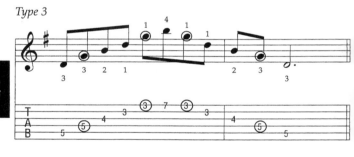

Type 4

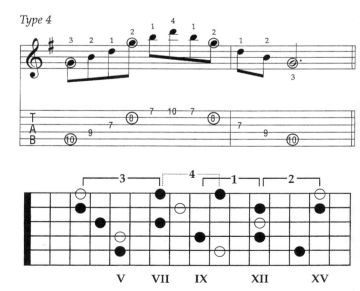

G6

Type 1

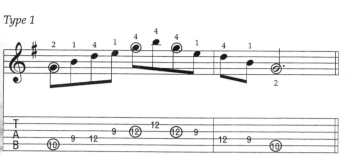

Type 2

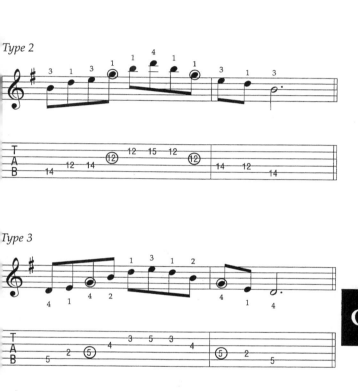

Type 3

G

Type 4

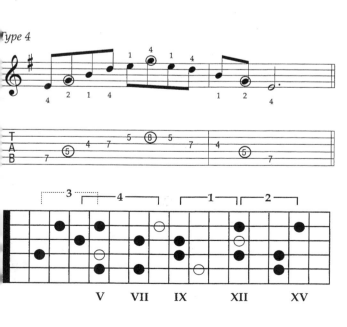

Gmaj7

Type 1

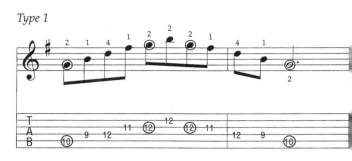

Type 2

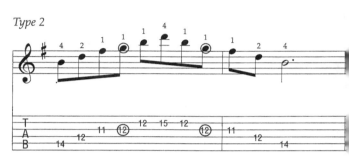

Type 3

Type 4

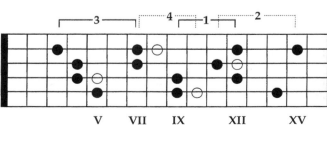

Gmaj9

Type 1

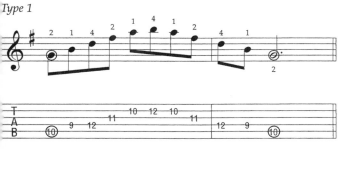

Type 2

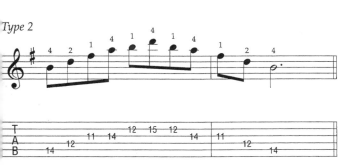

Type 3

G

Type 4

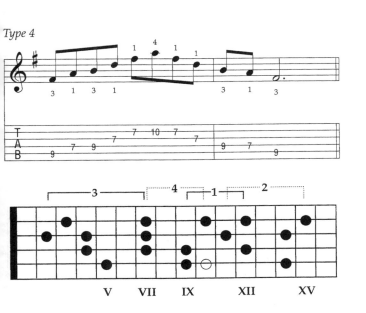

Gmaj9(♯11)

Type 1

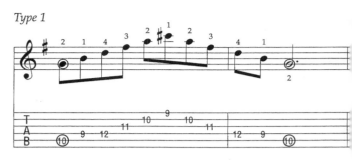

Type 2

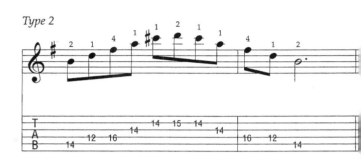

Type 3

Type 4

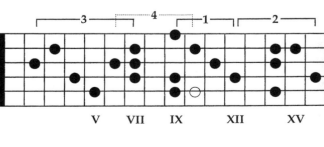

Gm

Type 1

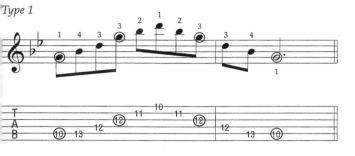

Type 2

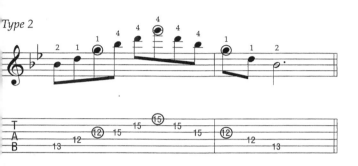

Type 3

G

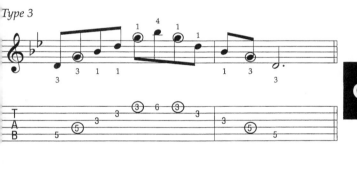

Type 4

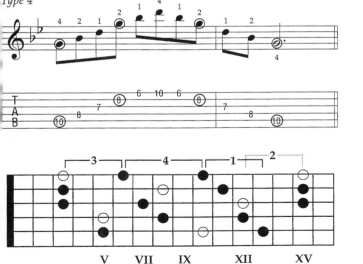

Gm6

Type 1

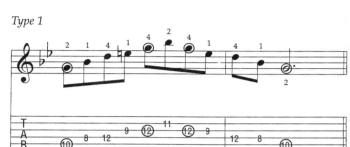

Type 2

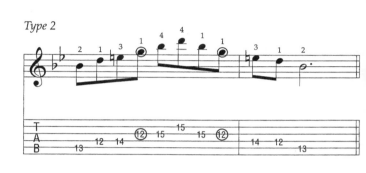

Type 3

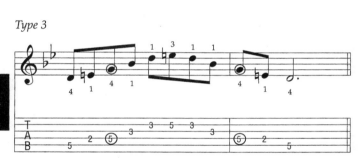

Type 4

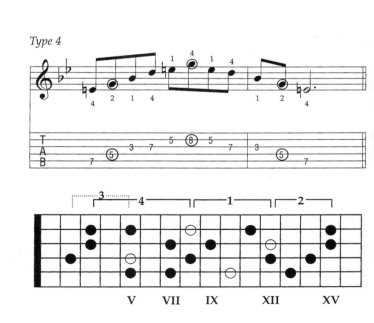

Gm7

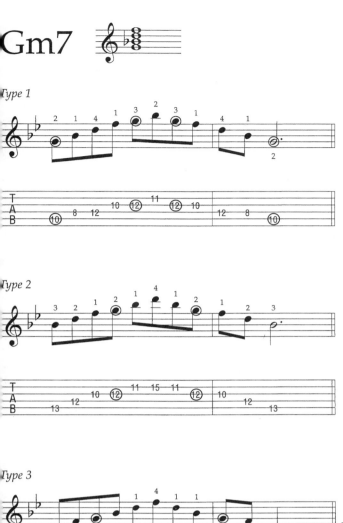

Type 1

Type 2

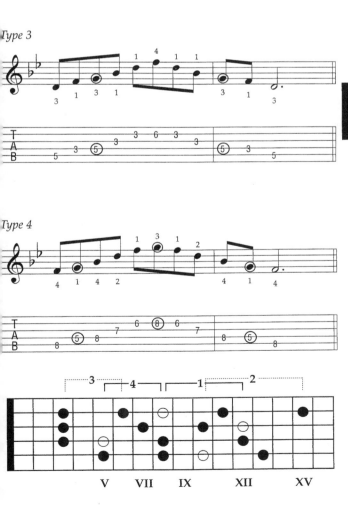

Type 3

G

Type 4

Gm9

Type 1

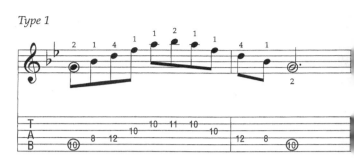

Type 2

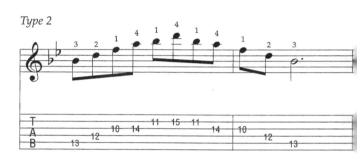

Type 3

G

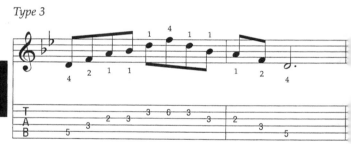

Type 4

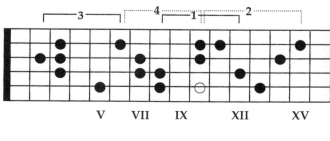

V   VII   IX   XII   XV

Gm11

Type 1

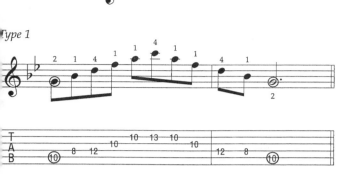

Type 2

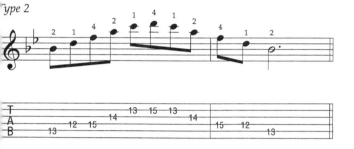

Type 3

G

Type 4

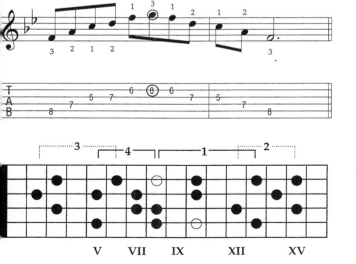

Gm(maj7)

Type 1

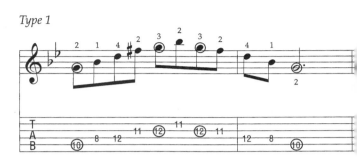

Type 2

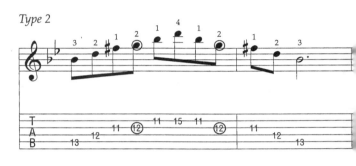

Type 3

Type 4

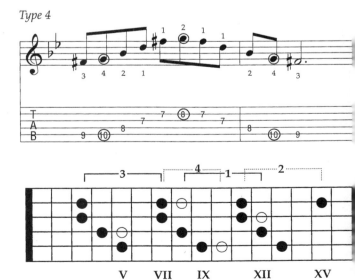

G7

Type 1

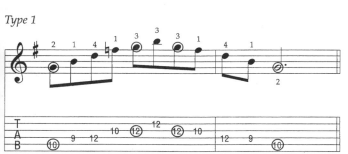

Type 2

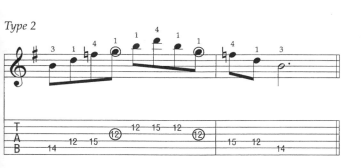

Type 3

G

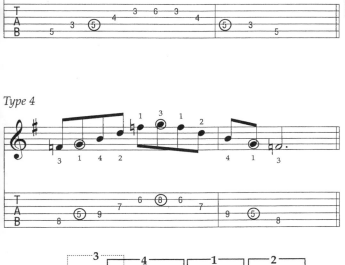

Type 4

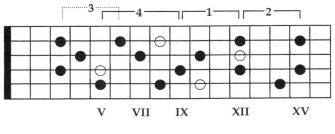

G9

Type 1

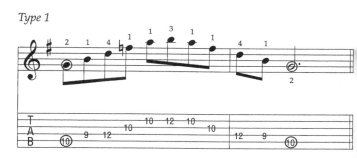

Type 2

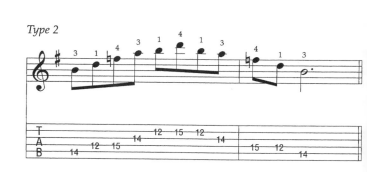

Type 3

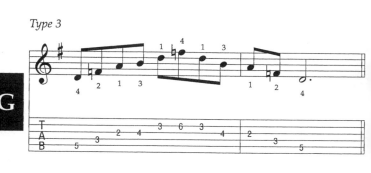

Type 4

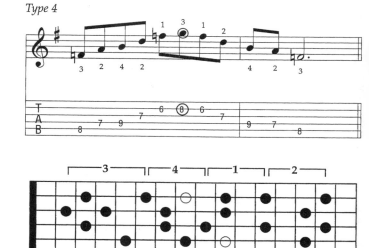

G7♭9

Type 1

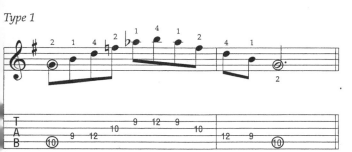

Type 2

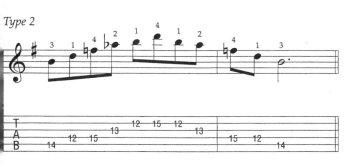

Type 3

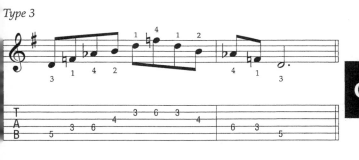

G

Type 4

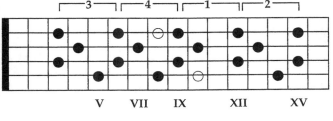

G7♯9

Type 1

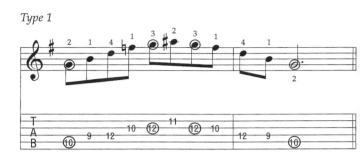

Type 2

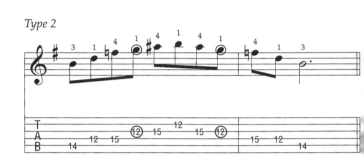

Type 3

Type 4

G9#11

Type 1

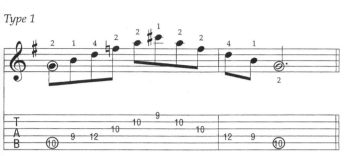

Type 2

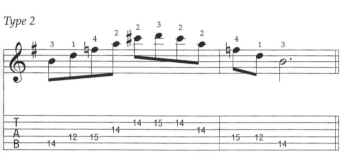

Type 3

G

Type 4

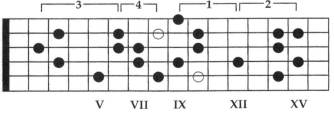

G7♭5

Type 1

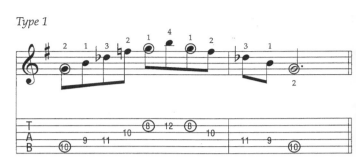

Type 2

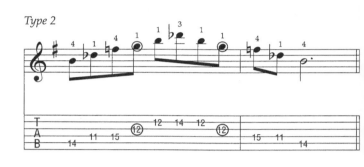

Type 3

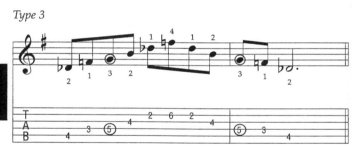

Type 4

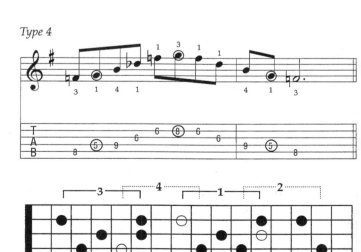

G7+

Type 1

Type 2

Type 3

Type 4

G

Gm7♭5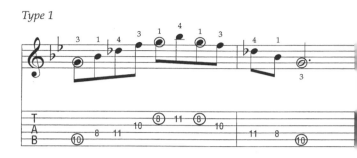

Type 1

Type 2

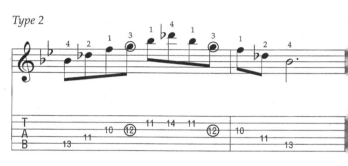

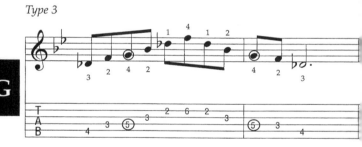

Type 3

Type 4

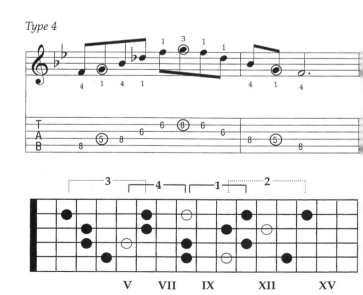

G°7

Type 1

Type 2

Type 3

G

Type 4

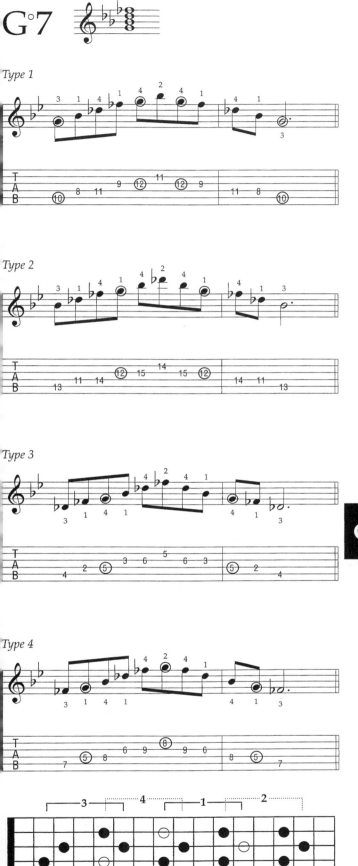

A♭

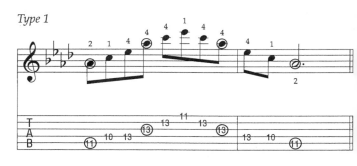

Type 1

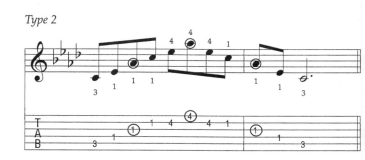

Type 2

Type 3

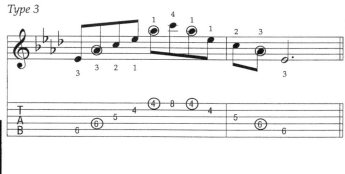

A♭
G♯

Type 4

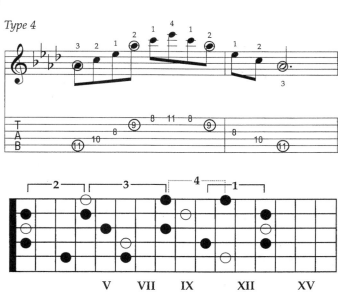

A♭6

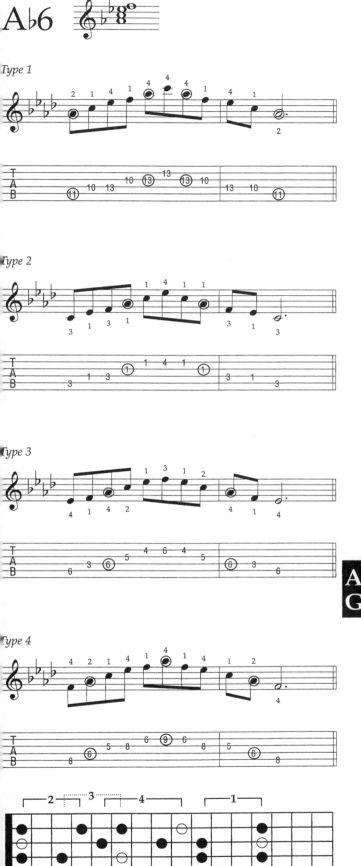

Type 1

Type 2

Type 3

Type 4

A♭maj7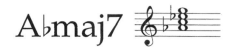

Type 1

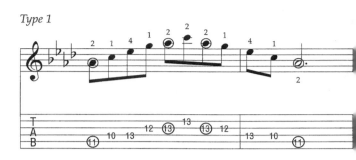

Type 2

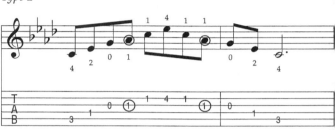

Type 3

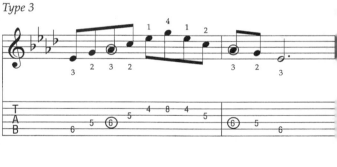

Type 4

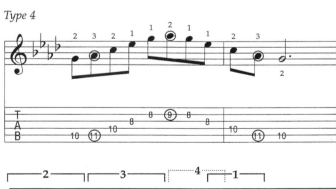

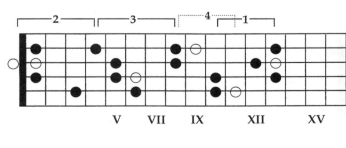

A♭maj9

Type 1

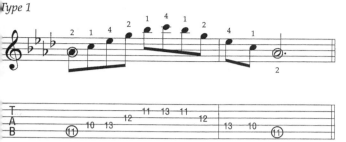

Type 2

Type 3

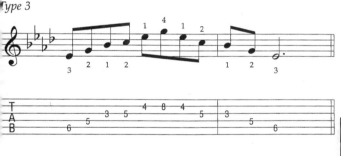

Type 4

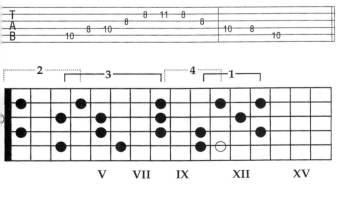

Abmaj9(#11)

Type 1

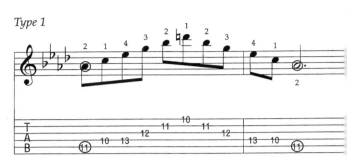

Type 2

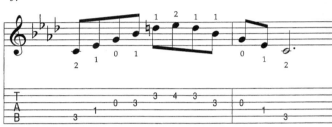

Type 3

Type 4

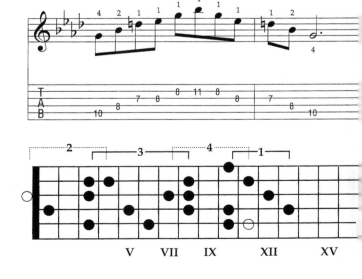

A♭m

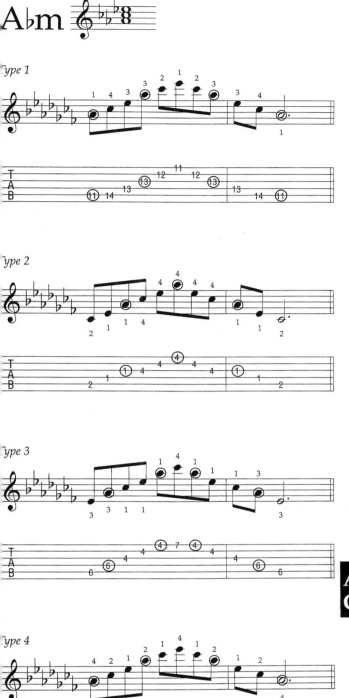

Type 1

Type 2

Type 3

Type 4

A♭
G#

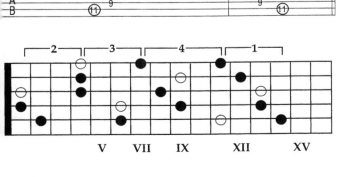

A♭m6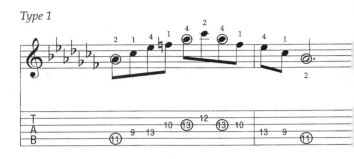

Type 1

Type 2

Type 3

Type 4

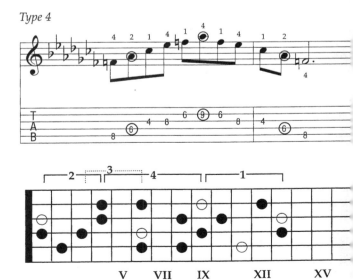

A♭m7

Type 1

Type 2

Type 3

Type 4

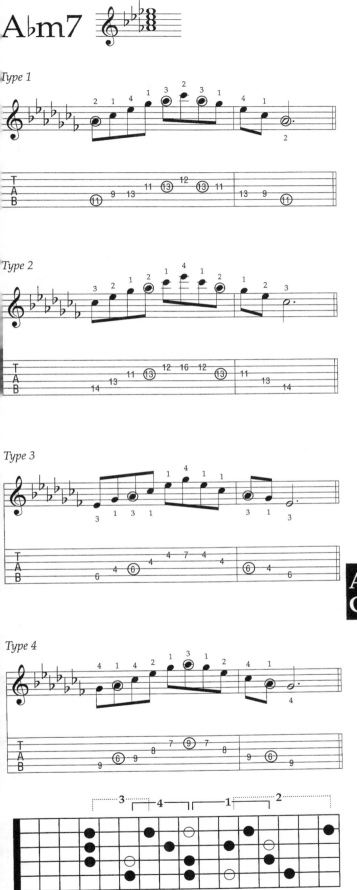

Abm9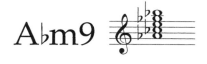

Type 1

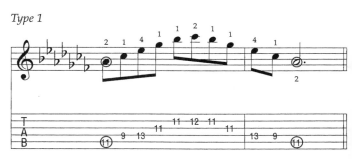

Type 2

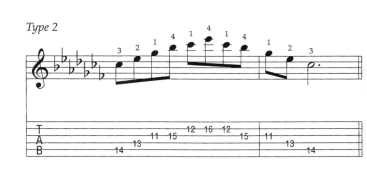

Type 3

Type 4

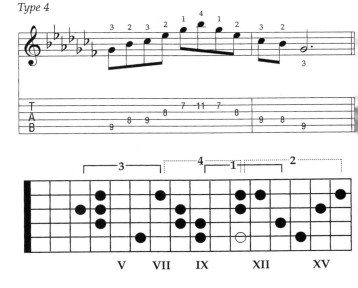

A♭m11

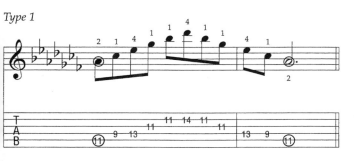

Type 1

Type 2

Type 3

A♭
G#

Type 4

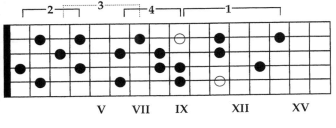

A♭m(maj7)

Type 1

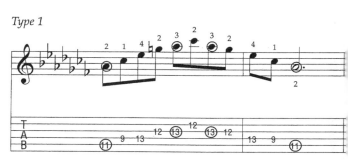

Type 2

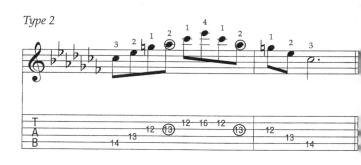

Type 3

Type 4

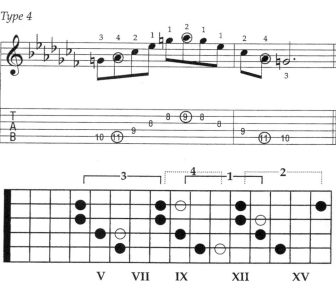

A♭7

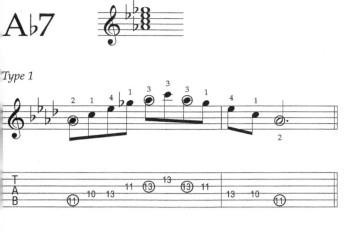

Type 1

Type 2

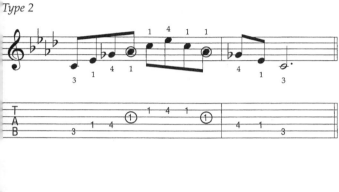

Type 3

Type 4

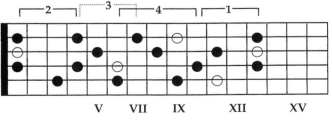

A♭9

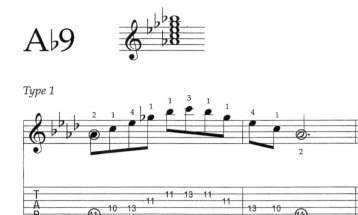

Type 1

Type 2

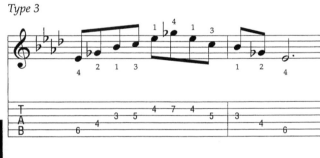

Type 3

Type 4

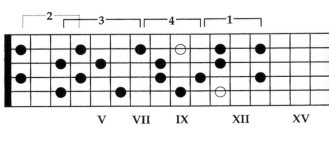

A♭7♭9

Type 1

Type 2

Type 3

Type 4

Ab7#9

Type 1

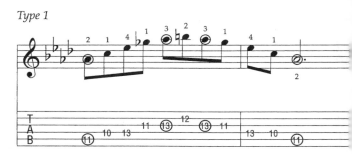

Type 2

Type 3

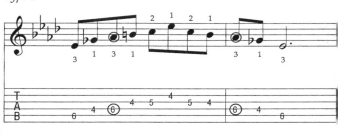

Type 4

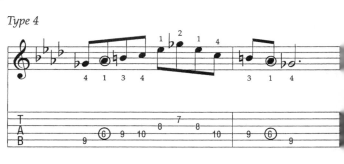

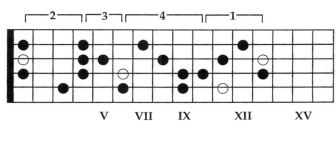

A♭9♯11

Type 1

Type 2

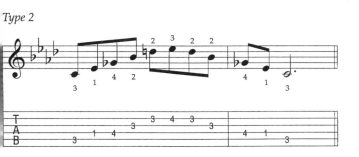

Type 3

Type 4

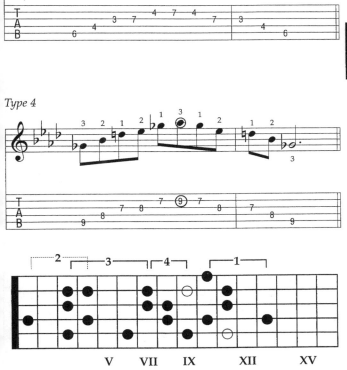

A♭7♭5

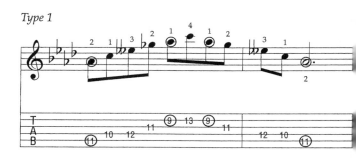

Type 1

Type 2

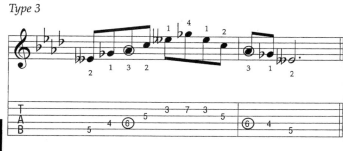

Type 3

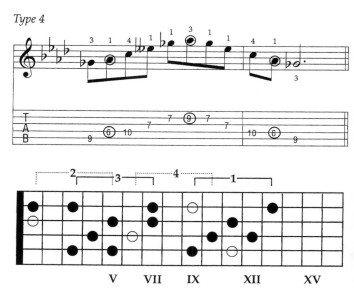

Type 4

A♭7+

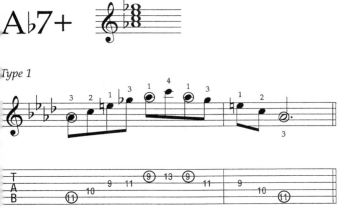

Type 1

Type 2

Type 3

Type 4

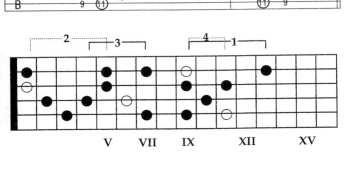

A♭m7♭5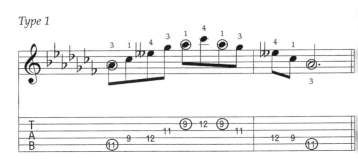

Type 1

Type 2

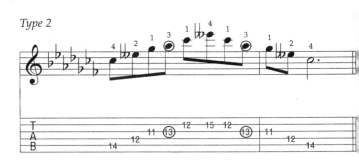

Type 3

Type 4

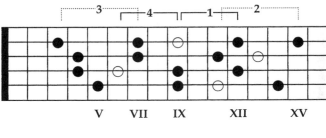

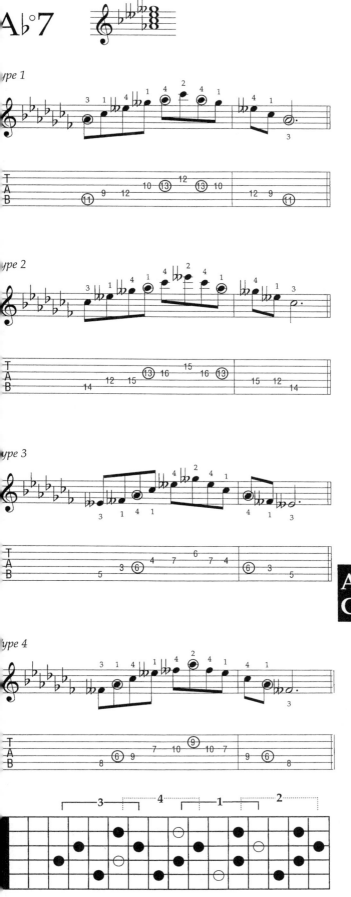

A

Type 1

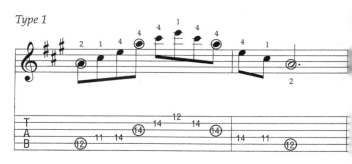

Type 2

Type 3

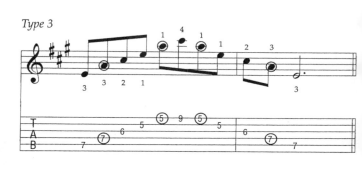

A

Type 4

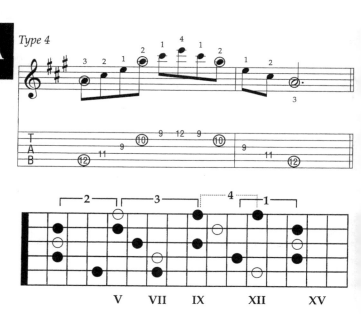

A6

A

Amaj7

Type 1

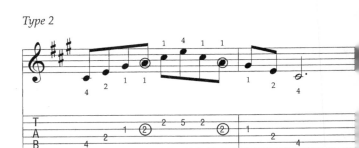

Type 2

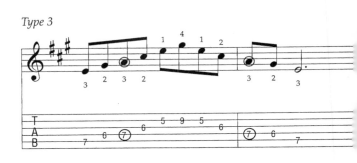

Type 3

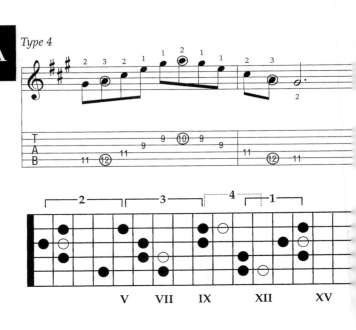

A

Type 4

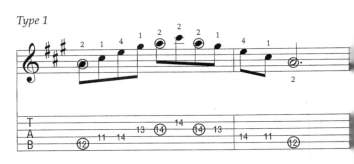

Amaj9

Type 1

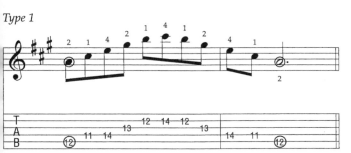

Type 2

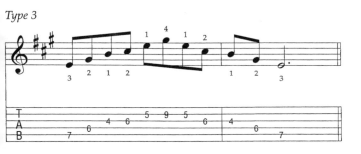

Type 3

Type 4

A

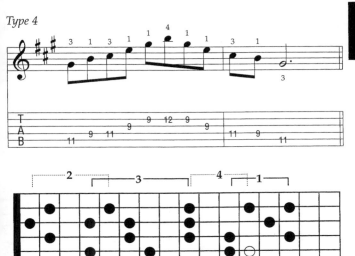

Amaj9(#11)

Type 1

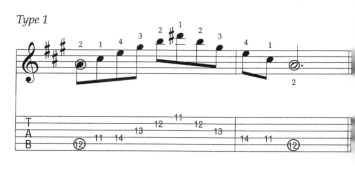

Type 2

Type 3

Type 4

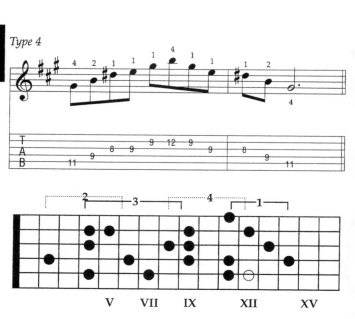

Am

Type 1

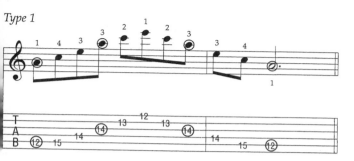

Type 2

Type 3

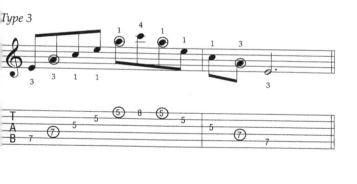

Type 4

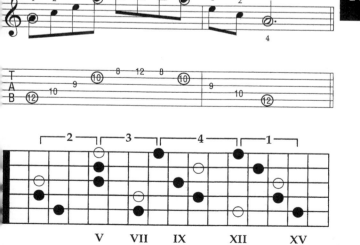

A

Am6

Type 1

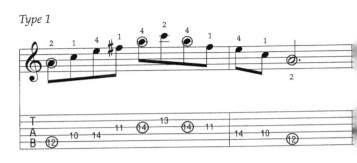

Type 2

Type 3

Type 4

A

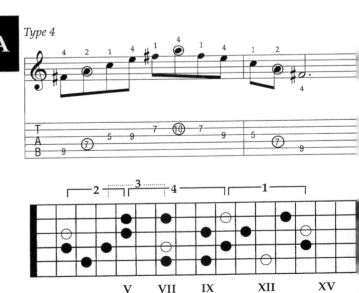

Am7

Type 1

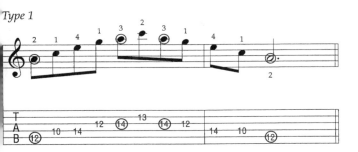

Type 2

Type 3

Type 4

A

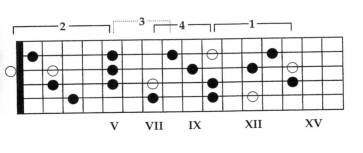

Am9

Type 1

Type 2

Type 3

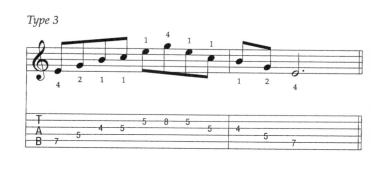

A

Type 4

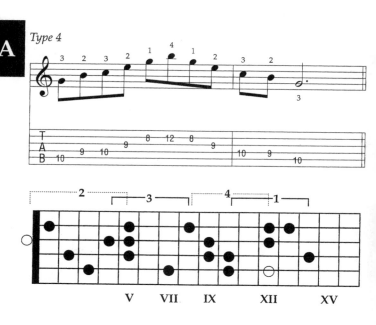

Am11

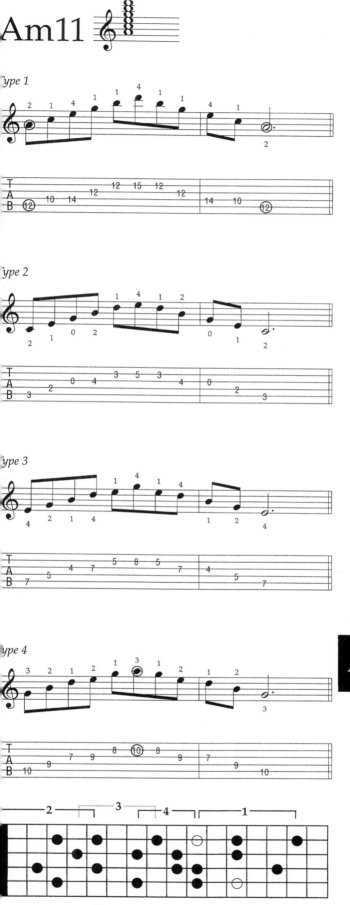

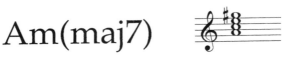

A MINOR

Am(maj7)

Type 1

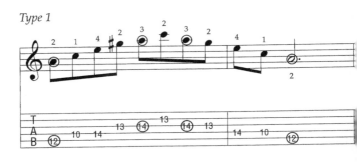

Type 2

Type 3

A

Type 4

A7

Type 1

Type 2

Type 3

Type 4

A

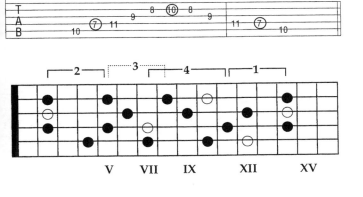

A9

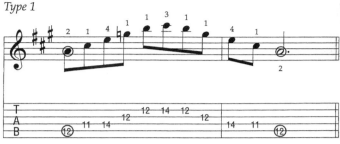

Type 1

Type 2

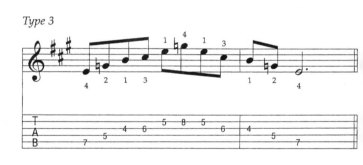

Type 3

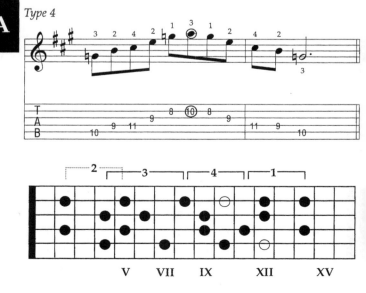

Type 4

A

A7♭9

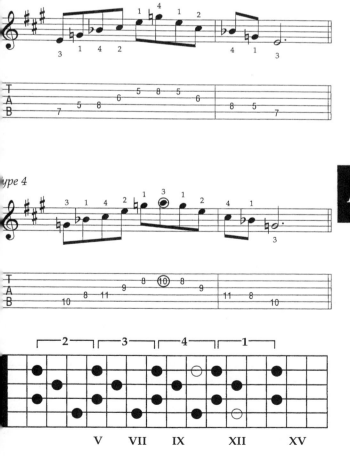

Type 1

Type 2

Type 3

Type 4

A

A7#9

Type 1

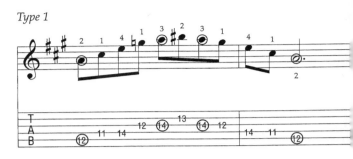

Type 2

Type 3

A

Type 4

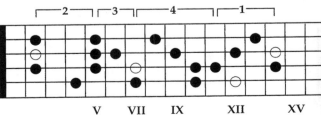

A9#11

Type 1

Type 2

Type 3

Type 4

A

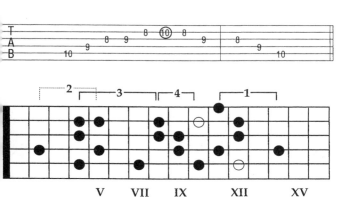

A7b5

Type 1

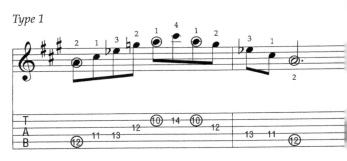

Type 2

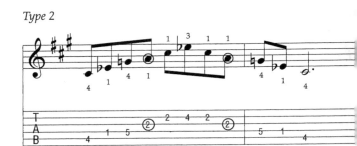

Type 3

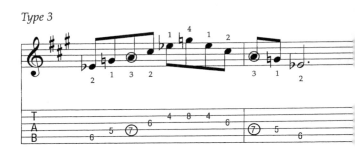

Type 4

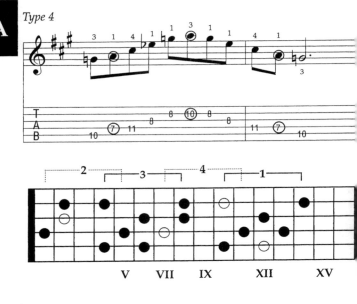

A7+

Am7♭5

Type 1

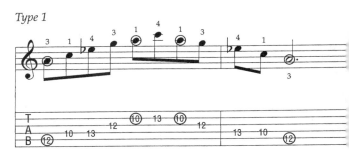

Type 2

Type 3

A

Type 4

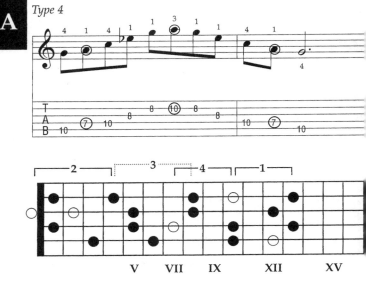

A°7

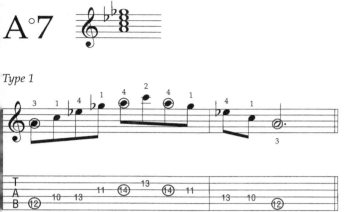

Type 1

Type 2

Type 3

Type 4

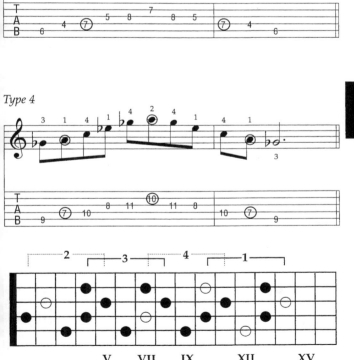

A

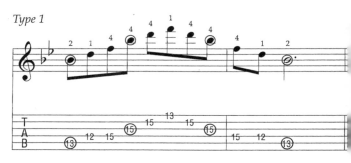

Type 1

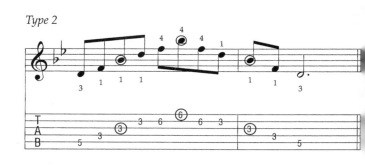

Type 2

Type 3

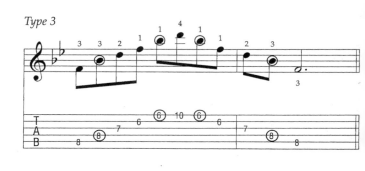

Type 4

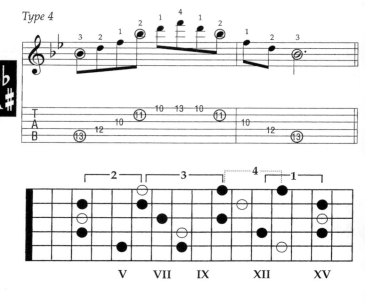

B♭6

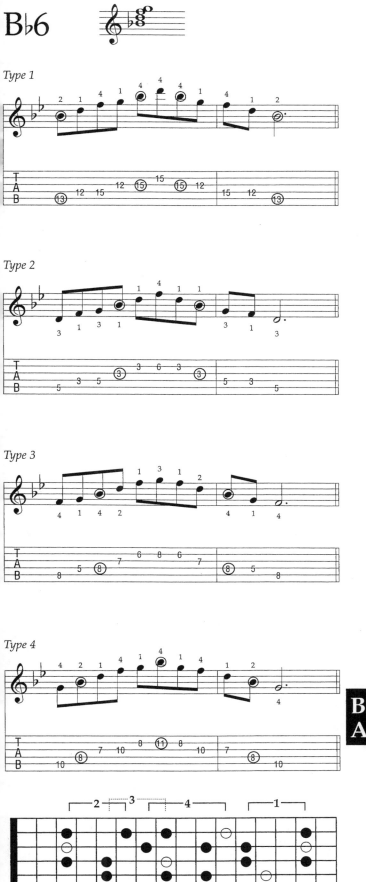

B♭maj7

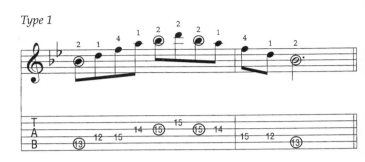

Type 1

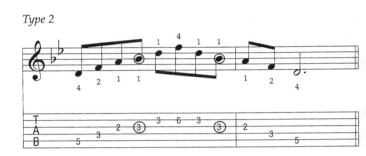

Type 2

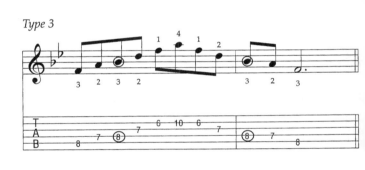

Type 3

Type 4

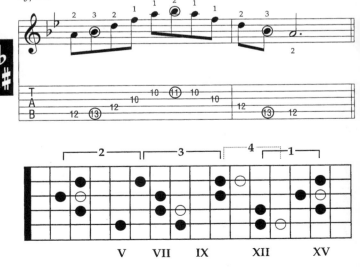

B♭maj9

Type 1

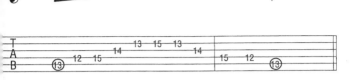

Type 2

Type 3

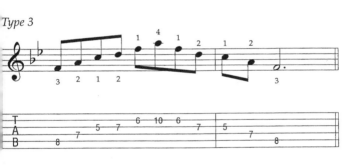

Type 4

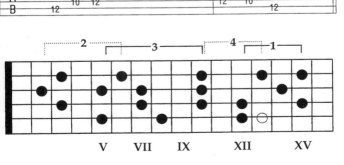

Bbmaj9(#11)

Type 1

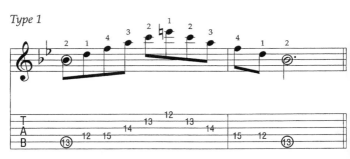

Type 2

Type 3

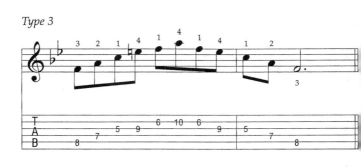

Type 4

Bb
A#

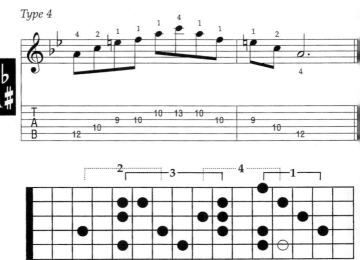

B♭m

Type 1

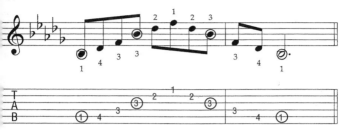

Type 2

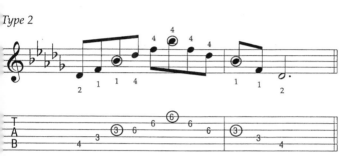

Type 3

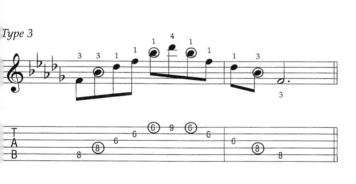

Type 4

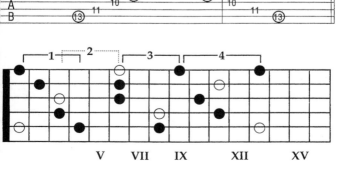

B♭m6

Type 1

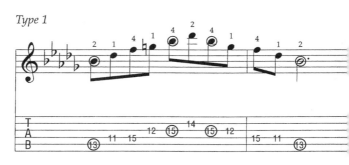

Type 2

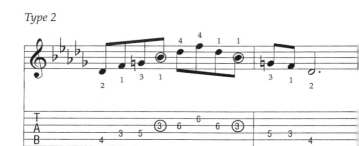

Type 3

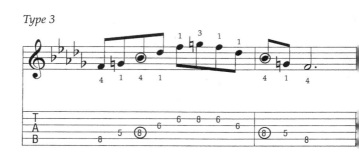

Type 4

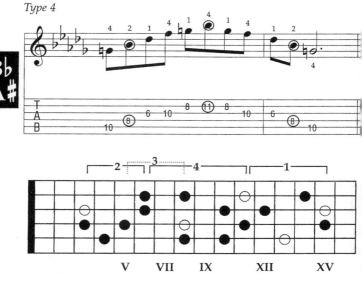

Bbm7

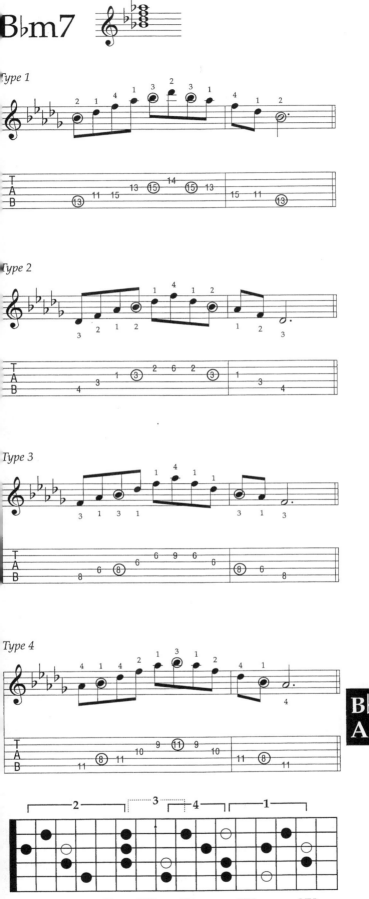

Type 1

Type 2

Type 3

Type 4

B♭m9

Type 1

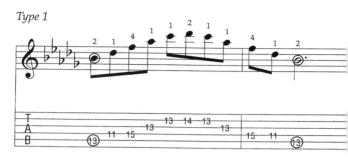

Type 2

Type 3

Type 4

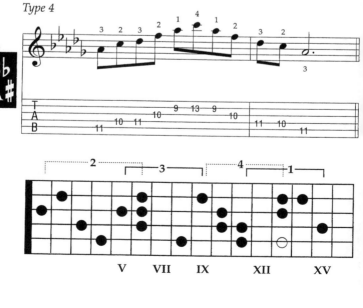

B♭
A♯

B♭m11

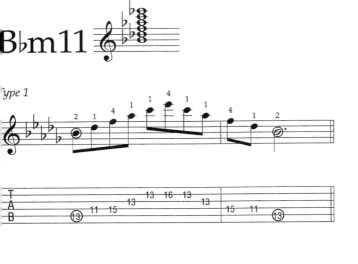

Type 1

Type 2

Type 3

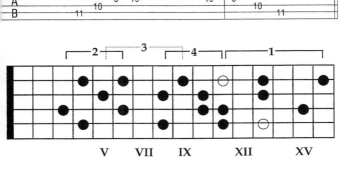

Type 4

B♭m(maj7)

Type 1

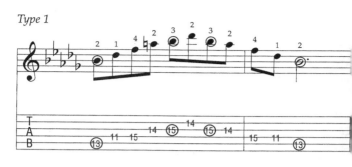

Type 2

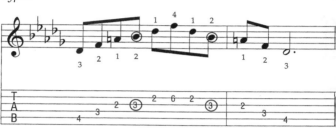

Type 3

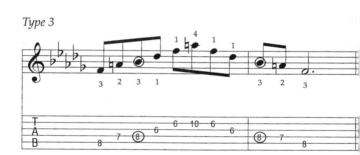

Type 4

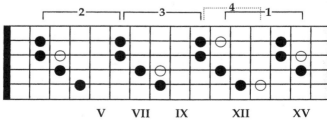

B♭7

Type 1

Type 2

Type 3

Type 4

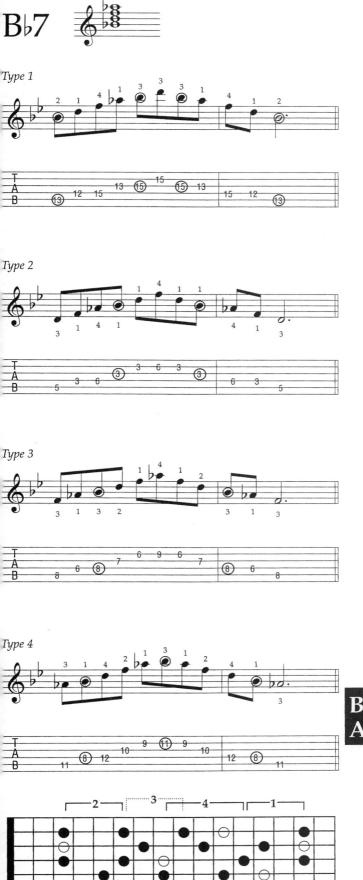

B♭9

Type 1

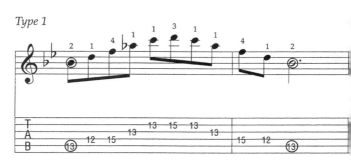

Type 2

Type 3

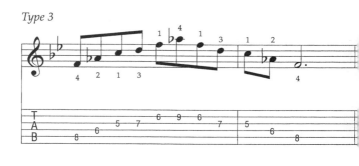

Type 4

B♭
A♯

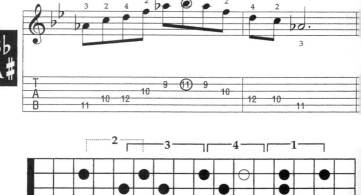

B♭7♭9

Bb7♯9

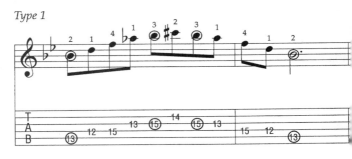

Type 1

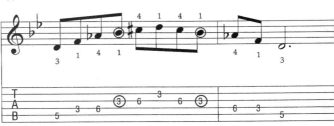

Type 2

Type 3

Type 4

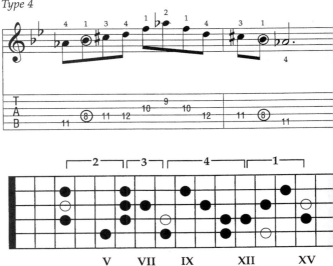

B♭9♯11

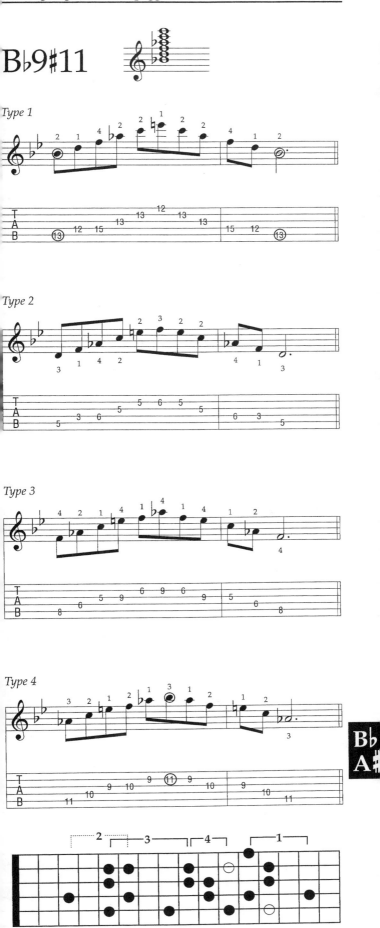

Bb7b5

Type 1

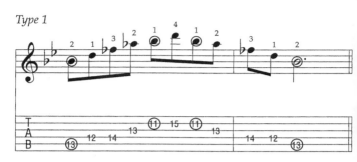

Type 2

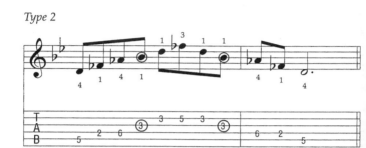

Type 3

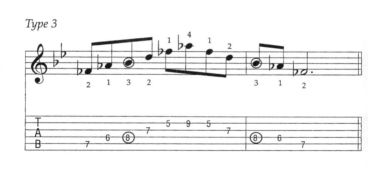

Type 4

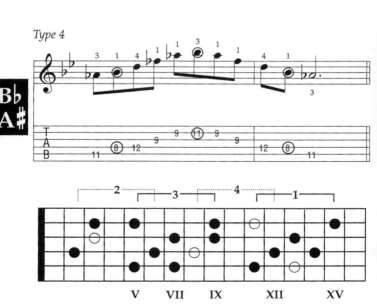

B♭7+

Type 1

Type 2

Type 3

Type 4

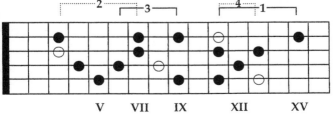

B♭
A#

B♭m7♭5

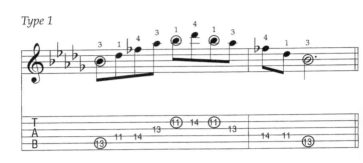

Type 1

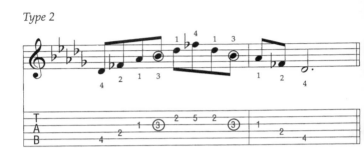

Type 2

Type 3

Type 4

B♭
A♯

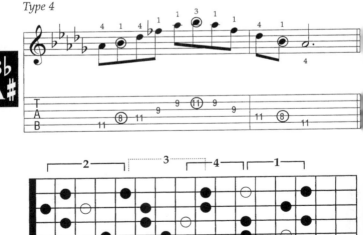

B♭°7

Type 1

Type 2

Type 3

Type 4

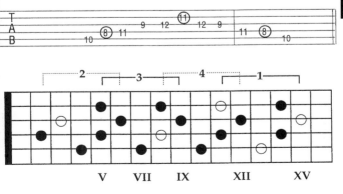

B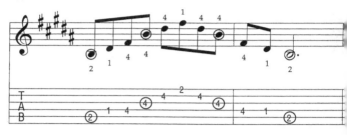

Type 1

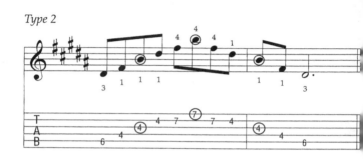

Type 2

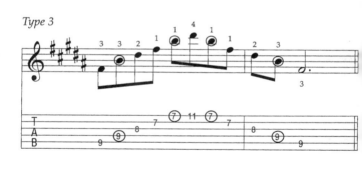

Type 3

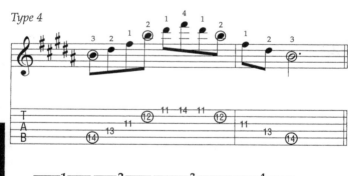

Type 4

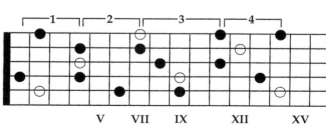

B

B6

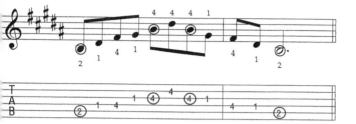

Type 1

Type 2

Type 3

Type 4

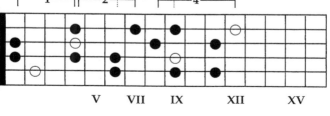

B

Bmaj7

Type 1

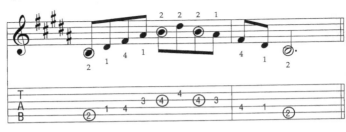

Type 2

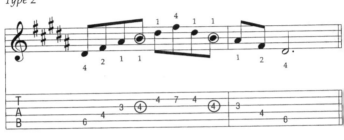

Type 3

Type 4

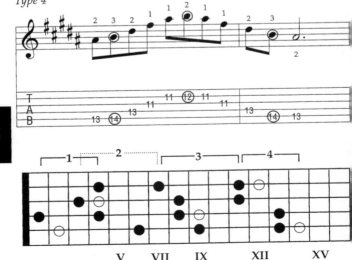

Bmaj9

Type 1

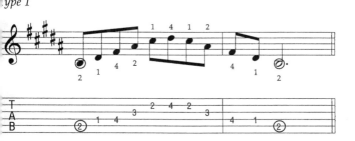

Type 2

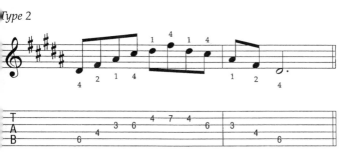

Type 3

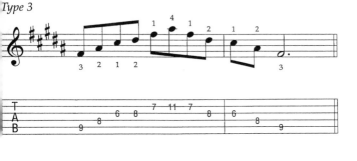

Type 4

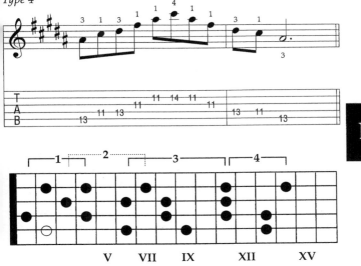

B

Bmaj9(♯11)

Type 1

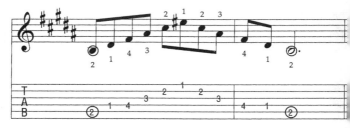

Type 2

Type 3

Type 4

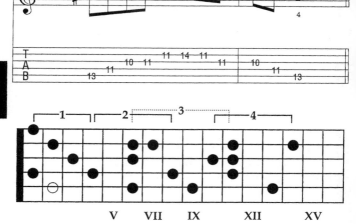

Bm

Type 1

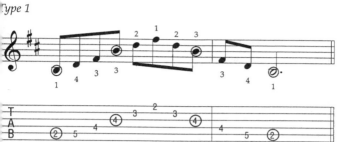

Type 2

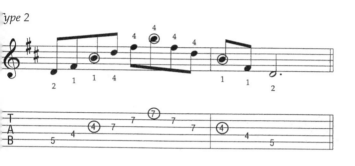

Type 3

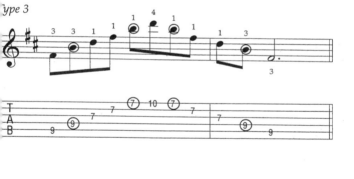

Type 4

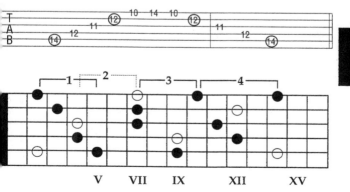

B

Bm6

Type 1

Type 2

Type 3

B

Type 4

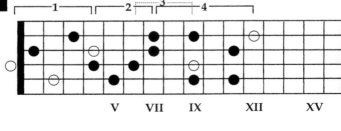

Bm7

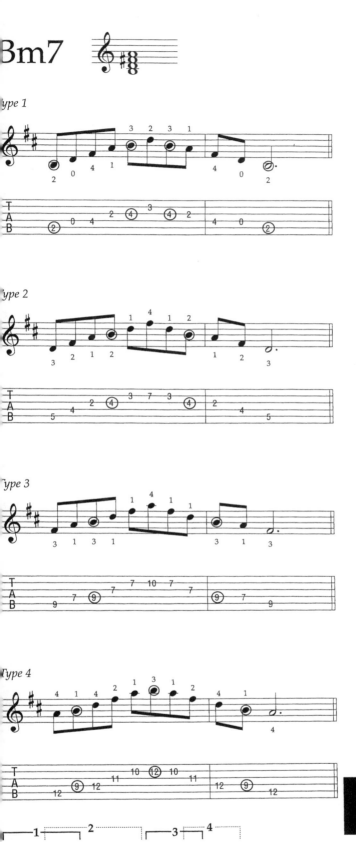

Bm9

Type 1

Type 2

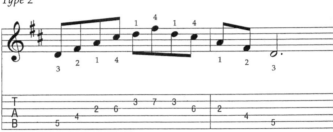

Type 3

Type 4

B

Bm11

Type 1

Type 2

Type 3

Type 4

B

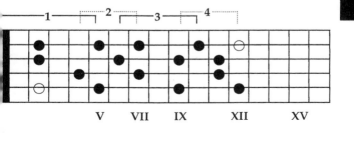

Bm(maj7)

Type 1

Type 2

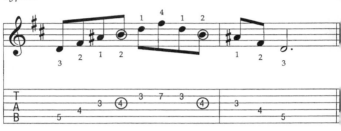

Type 3

Type 4

B

B7

Type 1

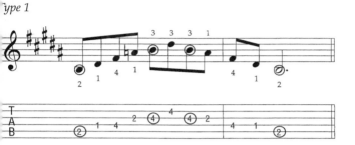

Type 2

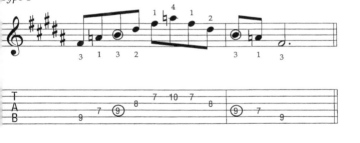

Type 3

Type 4

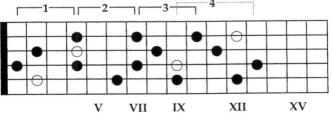

B

B9

Type 1

Type 2

Type 3

Type 4

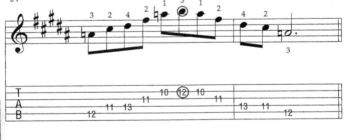

B

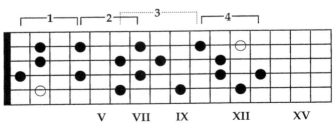

B7♭9

Type 1

Type 2

Type 3

Type 4

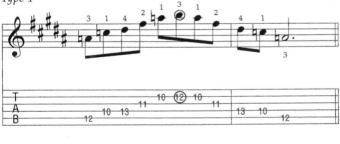

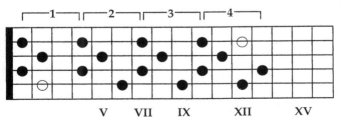

B7♯9

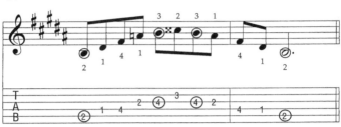

Type 1

Type 2

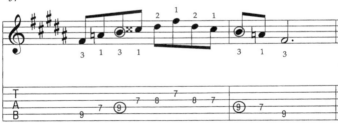

Type 3

Type 4

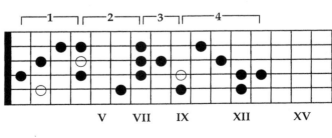

B9#11

Type 1

Type 2

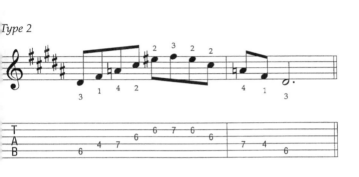

Type 3

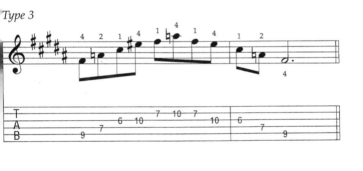

Type 4

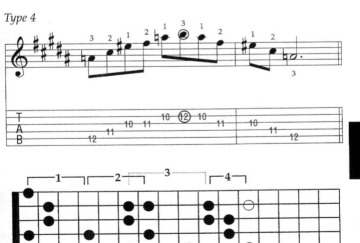

B

B7♭5

Type 1

Type 2

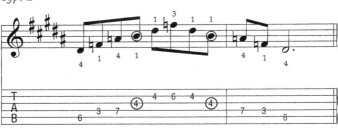

Type 3

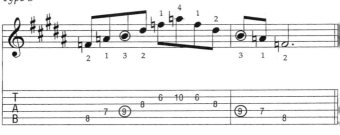

Type 4

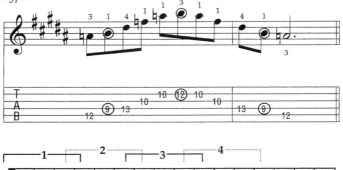

B7+

Type 1

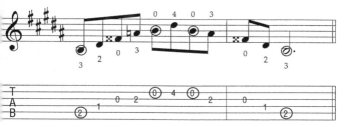

Type 2

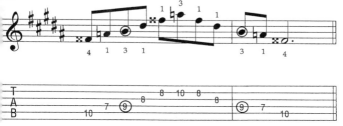

Type 3

Type 4

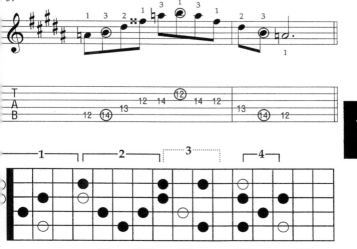

B

Bm7♭5

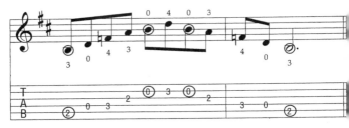

Type 1

Type 2

Type 3

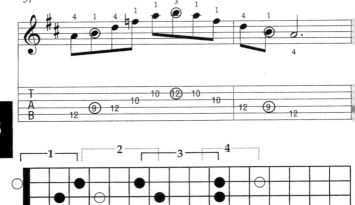

Type 4

B

B°7

Type 1

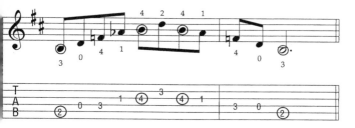

Type 2

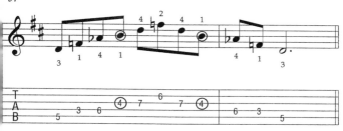

Type 3

Type 4

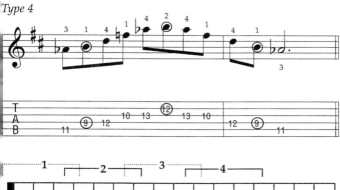

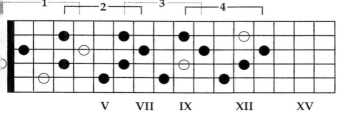

B